BUSINESS APPLICATIONS OF DECISION SCIENCES

Stephen Paranka

ASSOCIATE DEAN
COLLEGE OF BUSINESS
COLORADO STATE UNIVERSITY

FIRST EDITION

 PETROCELLI/CHARTER

NEW YORK 1975

Dedicated to Elsie and our four children:
Mike, Dave, Joan, and Julie.

Copyright © Mason/Charter Publishers, Inc. 1975

Published simultaneously in the United Kingdom by Mason/Charter
Publishers, Inc., London, England.

First Printing

Printed in the United States of America

Library of Congress Cataloging in Publication Data

Paranka, Stephen.
 Business applications of decision sciences.

 Includes bibliographical references and index.
 1. Decision-making--Mathematical models. 2. Electronic data processing--Decision-making. 3. Electronic
data processing--Business. I. Title.
HD69.D4P355   658.4'03   74-30138
ISBN 0-88405-302-4

Contents

Contents

Statement of Purpose

Utilization of quantitative techniques has become a vital element in modern business decision making. The advent of the computer has enabled decision makers to incorporate highly sophisticated quantitative techniques into the problem-solving procedure. Evidence of quantification exists in all basic functional activities of business. Therefore it is necessary for current and future managers to learn the fundamentals of relevant quantitative techniques and to understand how to apply these techniques in various business problem situations.

The purpose of this book is twofold: (1) to provide the reader with a fundamental understanding of computer operations and quantitative techniques useful in decision-making processes and (2) to present examples of how these quantitative techniques are applied in real business problem situations. The book should be useful as a text for an advanced undergraduate course or a graduate level course in business decision making. Another group that should benefit from studying the book is the large number of current managers in the business world who desire to advance their decision-making capability.

The first part of the book has three chapters designed to introduce the reader to an understanding of problem-solving processes and the general application of a computer in decision making. There is a discussion of the model approach to problem solving in Chapter 1. Chapter 2 outlines the fundamentals of computer operations and computer capability. The development of computer applications in decision making is covered in Chapter 3.

The next six chapters of the book include an explanation of specific quantitative techniques: first, to provide the reader with an understanding of the concepts involved and, second, to present pragmatic illustrations of how these quantitative techniques are applied in real business problem situations, particularly with the aid of a computer. The topics covered are Bayesian decision making in Chapter 4, linear programming in Chapter 5, queuing theory in Chapter 6, simulation in Chapter 7, Markov process in Chapter 8, and correlation and regression analysis in Chapter 9.

The final chapter in the book, Chapter 10, presents a look into the future of computer operations to indicate some of the innovations that are being developed to assist managers in future decision-making processes.

CHAPTER 1

Models and Analysis

ROLE OF THE BUSINESS MANAGER

The role of the business manager is basically that of a problem solver. He is the administrator of an organizational unit and has the fundamental responsibility to supervise labor, material, and capital in an optimal fashion toward the achievement of established objectives. A problem is present when the organizational unit is not performing as expected. The manager has several options: (1) ignore the problem, (2) ignore the facts and make an irrational decision, (3) resort to a random-choice process, or (4) use a rational process, combined with judgment, to reach a decision. The last option is the one that will receive primary attention in this text.

There are several bases for rational decision making: (1) experience, (2) intuition, or (3) systematic analysis. In the first procedure, the manager may have experienced a similar problem in the past: Given identical circumstances, he could apply a solution based on previous experience. Although the use of tested solutions is desirable, the opportunity to do so occurs infrequently. Not only do problem types change, but surrounding circumstances also change, making unwise the general use of past decisions.

Problem solving by intuition is associated with a "feeling" about a problem. A manager may arrive at a solution on the basis of a personal feeling that he has about the problem. Such an intuitive approach has the advantage of speed and economy. However, as the complexity of operations and the risk increase, decisions for action require more preparation. Systematic analysis, complemented by experience and intuition, is the recommended approach to problem solving in business, just as the scientific method is typically applied to problems in the natural sciences. Systematic analysis is a procedure whereby cause and effect relationships in a problem situation are studied. Ideally, some variable(s) in the system will be identifiable as the cause(s) of the underlying problem. An analysis of alternatives provides a basis for the manager's decision. One of the formal procedures for systematic analysis is the utilization of mathematical models.

DEFINITION OF A MATHEMATICAL MODEL

A model is a representation of a system in physical, verbal, or mathematical terms. A physical model, such as a model of a ship, is simply a representation of the physical properties of the actual object reduced or enlarged according to some proportional scale. A verbal model, such as a description of the solar system, abstracts the object or procedure into words. A mathematical model is a quantitative expression that indicates a functional relationship between relevant variables. The model may be a simple expression, citing the effect of one variable as a cause for change in a dependent variable as illustrated by a mathematical model showing the level of advertising expenditure as a cause effecting change in sales of a product. Given a problem in sales the manager can consider the advertising variable in the decision-making process. Most real business situations tend to be more complicated, requiring the application of sophisticated mathematical models. Instead of one variable, a typical mathematical model will contain several variables in a quantitative relationship to represent a cause for change. Chrysler Corporation executives had developed a forecasting model for the company's automobile sales which was based on 15 variables.[1] For the remainder of this text attention will be centered on the mathematical model.

FUNCTIONS OF A MATHEMATICAL MODEL

The use of a mathematical model is particularly helpful in the various stages of the problem-solving process, which are outlined in Figure 1–1. In the first stage, that of identifying the problem, the manager who uses a mathematical model approach becomes cognizant of the various issues of the problem. He learns of the relationships between factors in the model; these implications may not be completely evident from initial observations. For example, Kuehn's model, which is

---

[1] Sheehan, Robert. The price of success at Chrysler. *Fortune* 70(1965): 240.

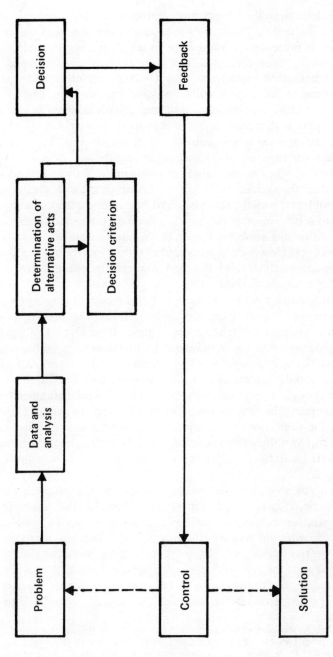

Figure 1–1.

designed to determine the advertising appropriation for a product, cites 10 significant variables.[2] Although the model at the time was still in the testing stage, it presented a framework in which managers could study relevant variables, even though a final solution was not developed.

The mathematical model provides a vehicle for clear and concise communications in the stage of collecting data and analysis. There is not the danger of mistaken interpretation of mathematical symbols as is true of many words in verbal models. Various individuals working together as researchers, mathematical specialists, and managers thus have a common language for their interpersonal communications.

Not only is the mathematical model more universal and less ambiguous than the verbal, it can also be manipulated with greater ease. Complex problems, which previously had been impractical or too time consuming to solve, can now be quickly solved on high speed computers. The result is that the problem solver can consider detailed analysis of more alternatives. However, the computer should not be regarded as a replacement for analysts and decision makers; computers are not a substitute for clear, hard thinking.

A possible danger is the development of a model that is beyond the comprehension of the user. Experience has indicated that erudite models can represent a barrier to manager application. John D. C. Little points out that it is important for a manager to understand a mathematical model so that he knows what to expect from it.[3] For maximum benefit the manager should understand the capabilities and limitation of the model, even though he may not fully understand the mathematical basis. It is recommended that the manager be involved in the model-building process. At the same time the model should not be so simplified as to omit significant variables of the problem situation. It is important that a model be tested carefully to determine if all significant variables have been included.

The analysis step tells the manager what consequences to expect from the various courses of action available. In the example of advertising appropriation the different courses of action would be represented by different budget amounts. Chosen decision criteria, such company objectives as sales, profit, market share, or social responsibility, and the manager's analysis of alternative acts will indicate the desired decision. Assume that the manager wants to retain a market share of 15 percent for a given product and that sales are directly correlated to the

---

[2] Kuehn, Alfred A. Models for the budgeting of advertising. In *Models, Measurement and Marketing*, ed. Peter Langhoff. Englewood Cliffs, N.J.: Prentice-Hall, 1965 (p. 128).

[3] Little, John D. C. Models and managers: The concept of a decision calculus. *Management Science*, 16(April, 1970): B-467.

size of the advertising budget. Then the manager can select the alternative act that meets his objective. The manager should be careful to consider all of the viable alternatives, since one of the most serious shortcomings in the decision-making process is the failure of the manager to do this.[4]

After the desired alternative has been selected and implemented, the mathematical model permits a follow-up analysis through a form of feedback procedure, such as posttesting. By comparing the follow-up results with some established control, which should be representative of his objectives, the manager can determine whether the problem appears to be solved by his action or if a problem still exists. In the example of determining advertising appropriation, the manager can readily determine from product sales figures whether his market share objective is being met.

Companies in which models are utilized in formal decision making appear to be more successful than other companies. A recent survey of 320 companies in the United States clearly indicated that companies which use models in a formal manner have grown more rapidly than companies which do not.[5]

DEVELOPMENT OF A MATHEMATICAL MODEL

A manager must balance the degree of realism and accuracy with the degree of complexity in developing a mathematical model so that the model is pragmatically applicable. The more realistic and accurate the model, the more complicated it tends to be. A model analysis that is beyond comprehension is not very helpful in the problem-solving procedures.

Model development can be traced through four phases: (1) problem formulation, (2) construction, (3) validation, and (4) solution of problem.

Problem Formulation

The effectiveness of the solution depends to a great extent on the effectiveness of the problem formulation. Simply to state the problem as a situation of declining sales is being too general. Assuming that the sales drop is significant, and not just a function of an economic recession, the manager should analyze the situation to pinpoint the problem more

---

[4] King, Peter. *Quantitative Analysis for Marketing Management*. New York: McGraw-Hill, 1967 (p. 16).

[5] Jackson, R. P. Improved management decision making through the use of business models. *Director*, 23(January, 1971): 73.

specifically. The following problem cycle framework is useful in analyzing a sales decline.

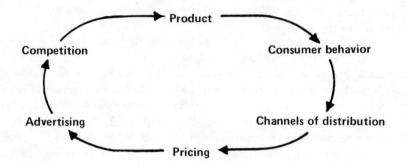

Each of the variables should be examined for its interrelationship to the reduction of sales until one or more can be selected as the specific problem.

Construction of a Mathematical Model

A mathematical model may be constructed either by abstraction or realization.[6] In the abstraction approach, one observes real world phenomena and develops a model patterned after the observations. In the realization approach, on the other hand, one begins with an abstract notion of what the real world phenomenon is and then compares the model to observations of reality. In each case the model can be refined until it represents the desired level of sophistication for the user.

In constructing a mathematical model via the abstraction method, empirical data are the basis for the creative effort, as shown in Figure 1–2. The empirical data can be obtained from existing records such as population census data or from primary research such as utilizing an original survey. In both approaches sound research techniques must be followed. Bias should be avoided and data should be relevant and reliable. Some factors to be considered in primary research are (1) appropriate data-collection instruments, (2) proper sample size, (3) valid sampling procedure, and (4) appropriate interviewing techniques. Marketing research agencies that specialize in primary research are available to perform contract studies for firms in need of this service.

After the data are collected, the model builder can analyze them to

---

[6] Lazer, William. The role of models in marketing. *Journal of Marketing*, 26(April, 1962): 10.

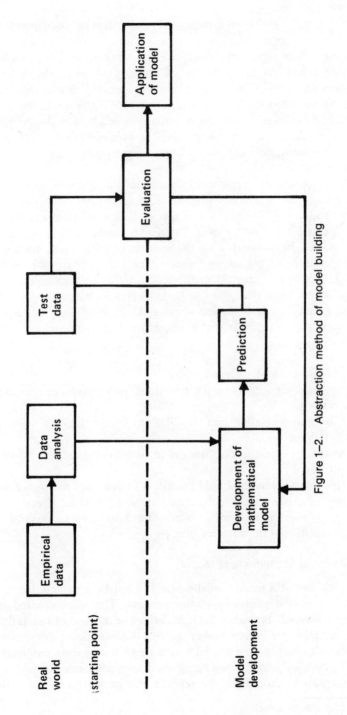

Figure 1–2. Abstraction method of model building

9

determine if functional relationships exist. Various statistical techniques lend themselves to an analysis of data. One example is stepwise regression analysis in which independent variables are compared to a dependent variable, such as sales, to determine if the relationship of any variable(s) to sales is significant, as usually noted by a high coefficient of correlation result. A preliminary step in model building would be to extract a mathematical expression of significant independent variables as a predictor of sales in the above analysis.

In the realization approach, the model builder selects a particular mathematical model already formulated (such as one of those described in later chapters of this book) and applies it to a problem situation. This latter approach is of general benefit to today's managers. Many problems can be tackled with the assistance of known mathematical models without necessitating the construction of a special model. As shown in Figure 1–3, an existing model can either be applied directly to a problem or be refined slightly to fit a special problem.

Regardless of construction approach, the developed mathematical model should include certain characteristics if it is to assist a manager in making decisions:[7]

1. Simplicity—ease of understanding
2. Robustness—designed so model does not produce unreasonable answers
3. Ease of control—user can manipulate input data to vary model computations
4. Adaptability—capability of model to be adjusted as new information is collected
5. Completeness—model should include all important relationships even if some of them require subjective estimates of their effect
6. Easy to communicate with—user should be able to control inputs easily and to obtain answers quickly

Validation of a Mathematical Model

To be useful a model must work. It must be a vehicle for accurate predictions in the problem-solving process. Therefore created models must be validated. Probably the most effective method of validation is to test a model's predictive power against known data; for example, a product sales-forecasting model could be tested against empirical sales data of previous years before being used to predict sales of future years. A mathematical model can be refined and improved in the validation

---

[7] Little, *op. cit.*, p. B-466.

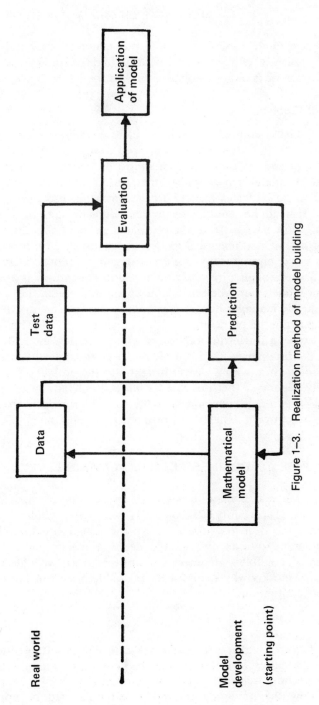

Figure 1–3. Realization method of model building

11

stage. If the model does not work, the manager must refine it or ultimately reject it. Otherwise he would be like the soldier who believes that everyone else is out of step, not him, and the model is not beneficial.

Solution of Problem

The model is applied to a real problem in the last phase of model development. With the advent of high speed computers, it usually takes a very short period of time for a manager to obtain a solution to a mathematical model that is applied to a real problem. A manager need not feel that he is delegating his decision-making responsibility to the computer. Instead, he should consider himself as being in the position of demanding explanations from the computer. A significant advantage of the use of on-line mathematical models being processed through remote terminals to a computer is that the user can gain perception as to how the model works through direct experience. An illustration is the use of simulation models described in a later chapter. Through the simulation framework, the manager has an opportunity to experiment with various inputs, following the procedure of "If ... , what then." Seldom should a manager expect a single-run solution of a mathematical model to provide him with the final answer to his problem. A mathematical model should at least provide him with a clearer insight into the problem. Further, the model may generate other possible variables to include in the analysis. The ideal situation is one in which the model provides a basis from which his executive judgment can proceed to a decision.

APPROACHES TO BUSINESS DECISION MAKING

A decision maker may be operating in any one of three different environments: (1) certainty, (2) risk, or (3) uncertainty. Under conditions of certainty, the decision maker knows the actual situation that will occur; under conditions of risk, the decision maker has probability knowledge of possible outcomes; but under uncertainty, he has little knowledge or no knowledge about the probable effects of the variables in a problem situation.

Certainty

The decision maker can easily evaluate the payoff of alternative actions in a situation of certainty since he knows the state of nature that will occur and can select the best course of action. A later chapter will illustrate how the linear programming technique can be applied to maximize the payoff in a complicated problem under certainty.

Risk

The decision maker has a more difficult task in a situation of risk. He can obtain a measure of the probabilities that each of the various states of nature will occur, based on deductive reasoning or empirical evidence. In the former situation he knows the characteristics of the eventuality of occurrence of each state of nature in advance; for example, the probability of a fair coin toss resulting in heads with $P = 0.5$. Empirical evidence assumes that a sufficient number of past experiences are known to provide a measure for the probabilities of occurrence of each state of nature. Knowing the probabilities, the decision maker can calculate the different payoffs of each alternative action and can select the best action. However, there is a measurable risk of loss involved in the decision, since the eventual occurrence of the state of nature is not known. A manager may be able to transfer the risk element as in the practice of buying some form of insurance; fire insurance, for instance, transfers a risk that is prohibitive for his company to an insurance company that can collect sufficient premiums to absorb occasional losses. The insurance company does not know which individual companies will be involved in a damage claim. Instead the company knows what percent of firms is likely to have losses, and insurance rates are based on actuarial tables of past experience of claims.

The manager assumes the possibility of loss in other situations of risk. A justification for profit in business operations is the degree of risk involved: The greater the risk, the greater should be the profit. The risk–profit relationship is then an encouragement to businessmen to take greater risks, which should result in greater innovation and progress.

Uncertainty—Partial Knowledge

Decision making under uncertainty is the most difficult situation, but also the most typical in business operations. Despite limited knowledge or a lack of any knowledge about the outcome of the problem variable, the manager is still expected to make a decision. Fortunately, some mathematical and statistical concepts have been developed in recent years to assist him in arriving at effective decisions. In the case of partial knowledge the decision maker can apply the Bayesian statistical concept which is his subjective estimate of a priori probability, an estimate of chance occurrence of a state of nature in an environment of uncertainty. A manager establishes a personal list of probabilities to the occurrence of various states of nature to determine the expected payoff amounts. His decision will be based on the results as explained in a later chapter on Bayesian decision making.

Uncertainty—No Knowledge

There are a number of criteria that can be used as a basis for decision making in a situation in which there is a lack of knowledge in a problem situation. Each of the criteria has a logical foundation to serve as a rationale for its use. However, each of the criteria also has definite limitations, precluding the general acceptance of any one. Therefore the decision maker must first choose the criterion and second select the best action on the basis of that criterion. The criteria include (1) the maximax criterion, (2) the Wald (maximin) criterion, (3) the minimax criterion, and (4) the Laplace criterion.

The maximax criterion. The decision maker makes a choice of the action with the maximum payoff among the outcomes associated with alternative actions. He selects that act which is associated with the largest return. Applying the maximax criterion to Table 1–1, the decision maker would select Act A_1:"bid high" because this act produces the largest available return, that is, $75,000. Rationale for this approach is that the decision maker would not have missed an opportunity for a larger payoff regardless of the outcome. The maximax approach is the most optimistic procedure, reflecting a "go for broke" attitude by the decision maker. In the data shown in Table 1–1, as in most business situations, the selected act based on the use of the maximax criteria could result in a very low payoff if the optimum state of nature does not occur. The payoff for Act A_1 and N_1 is zero, whereas the payoff for the worst possible outcome associated with Act A_2 is $30,000 and with Act A_3 is $35,000.

TABLE 1–1

| | State of Nature | |
Acts	N_1: Competitor A will bid	N_2: Competitor A will not bid
A_1: Bid high	0	$75,000
A_2: Bid medium	$30,000	60,000
A_3: Bid low	35,000	35,000

The Wald (maximin) criterion. The decision maker makes a choice of the act with the largest minimum payoff among the outcomes associated with alternative actions. Applying the maximin criterion, he would determine the payoffs of each of the acts under different states of nature, observe the smallest payoff of each act, and select the largest among these minimum outcomes. The rationale for this approach is that the decision maker is *guaranteed* at least the maximin result, regardless of the state of nature that prevails, whereas selection of one of the other acts could result in a lower payoff. In the illustrative data in Table 1–1, the decision maker would select Act A_3:"bid low" since the maximin payoff in this act is $35,000. The maximin approach represents a conservative procedure, because the decision maker foregoes the opportunity of possibly making larger payoffs as in Acts A_1 and A_2.

The minimax criterion. The decision maker makes a choice of the act with the smallest maximum loss among the outcomes associated with alternative actions. Applying the minimax criterion, he would first convert the payoff table to a regret table; that is, he would set the outcome for the act with the largest payoff for each state of nature as zero and the outcome of the other acts as the amount of difference (regret) between these other acts and the optimum act. The conversion of Table 1–1 into a regret table is shown in Table 1–2.

TABLE 1–2

Acts	State of Nature	
	N_1: Competitor A will bid	N_2: Competitor A will not bid
A_1: Bid high	$35,000	0
A_2: Bid medium	5,000	15,000
A_3: Bid low	0	40,000

Applying the minimax criterion, the decision maker would select Act A_2:"bid medium," since the maximum regret from this act is $15,000 whereas the maximum regret from Act A_1 is $35,000 and the maximum regret from Act A_3 is $40,000. The rationale is that the decision maker is minimizing the loss of opportunity with Act A_2 regardless of the state of nature outcome. The minimax approach is also a conservative procedure, but unlike the maximin approach, it does consider lost opportunity as a factor.

The Laplace criterion. The decision maker makes a choice of the act with the largest expected payoff assuming equal likelihood of occurrence of the various states of nature. Not knowing what the probability of occurrence is, he could assume equal probability for each state of nature outcome and thereby convert the problem into a risk situation. Using the data from Table 1–2, the decision maker can calculate expected payoffs as follows:

Act A_1: $\frac{1}{2}(0)$ + $\frac{1}{2}(\$75,000)$ = $\$37,500$
Act A_2: $\frac{1}{2}(\$30,000)$ + $\frac{1}{2}(\$60,000)$ = $\$45,000$
Act A_3: $\frac{1}{2}(\$35,000)$ + $\frac{1}{2}(\$35,000)$ = $\$35,000$

Applying the Laplace criterion, the decision maker would select Act A_2:"bid medium." Rationale for the decision is that the decision maker, in the absence of any information, should select the act with the largest payoff if all states of nature are assumed to have equal probabilities of occurrence. Many analysts decide that for lack of a better way, they should apply the Laplace criterion.[8]

---

[8] King, *op. cit.*, p. 59.

CHAPTER 2

Understanding Computer Operations

NEED FOR MANAGERS TO UNDERSTAND COMPUTER OPERATIONS

The computer is a fundamental tool in the complicated world of modern decision making with a basic capability to "crunch" massive amounts of data and to perform rapid computations. Its obvious limitation is being able to do only what it has been programmed to do. Quantitative specialists have been utilizing the power of computers in sophisticated problem-solving procedures for a number of years. Managers are in the process of discovering the merits of utilizing a computer. Terrance Hanold, president of the Pillsbury Company, has installed a computer terminal in the company's executive chart room to calculate effects of proposed acts.[1] He can learn immediately what will be the likely results from a proposal. It has been said that executives who do not learn computer applications might become the dinosaurs of the 1970s.[2]

The purpose of this chapter is to familiarize the reader with the physical makeup of a computer system and to introduce the programming procedure. It does not seem necessary for an executive to become a computer specialist, but there are certain fundamentals he should understand if he is to use a computer as a beneficial tool.

PHYSICAL MAKEUP OF A COMPUTER SYSTEM

A computer should really be considered in terms of a system, requiring an input component, a central processing unit, and an output

---

[1] Computers invade executive suites. *International Management,* 23(September, 1968): 52.
[2] Brown, W. F., and Hawkins, D. H. Remote access computing: The executive's responsibility. *Journal of Systems Management,* 23(June, 1972): 35.

component. There are alternative forms of input and output components. Input components may be the console typewriter, punched cards,
punched paper tape, magnetic tape, and the cathode-ray tube. Special
input components are magnetic-ink character recognition and optical
character recognition; both of these devices are used for reading printed
matter, for example, for checks.

A typical input form is by way of punched cards. How do punched
cards operate to provide information to the computer? First, cards are
punched according to the Hollerith punching system illustrated in Figure
2–1.

The computer reads each card through a card reader unit. The
information is converted into the binary system, which makes use of two
different digits rather than the ten that is used in the more common
decimal system. The binary system is based on the on/off electromagnetic coding in computer design, so that at any particular computer
location either there is a charge or there is no charge. When there is an
electromagnetic charge at a location, that condition is taken as 1 in the
binary system, whereas if no charge is present at a particular location,
that condition is taken as 0. The binary numbering system is thus based
on uses of the two digits 1 and 0. Larger numbers are portrayed by
extending the number of 1's and 0's that are used by continuing the
following sequence:

Decimal System	Binary System
0	0
1	1
2	10
3	11
4	100
5	101
6	110
7	111
8	1000
9	1001
10	1010
11	1011
12	1100
13	1101
14	1110
15	1111
16	10000

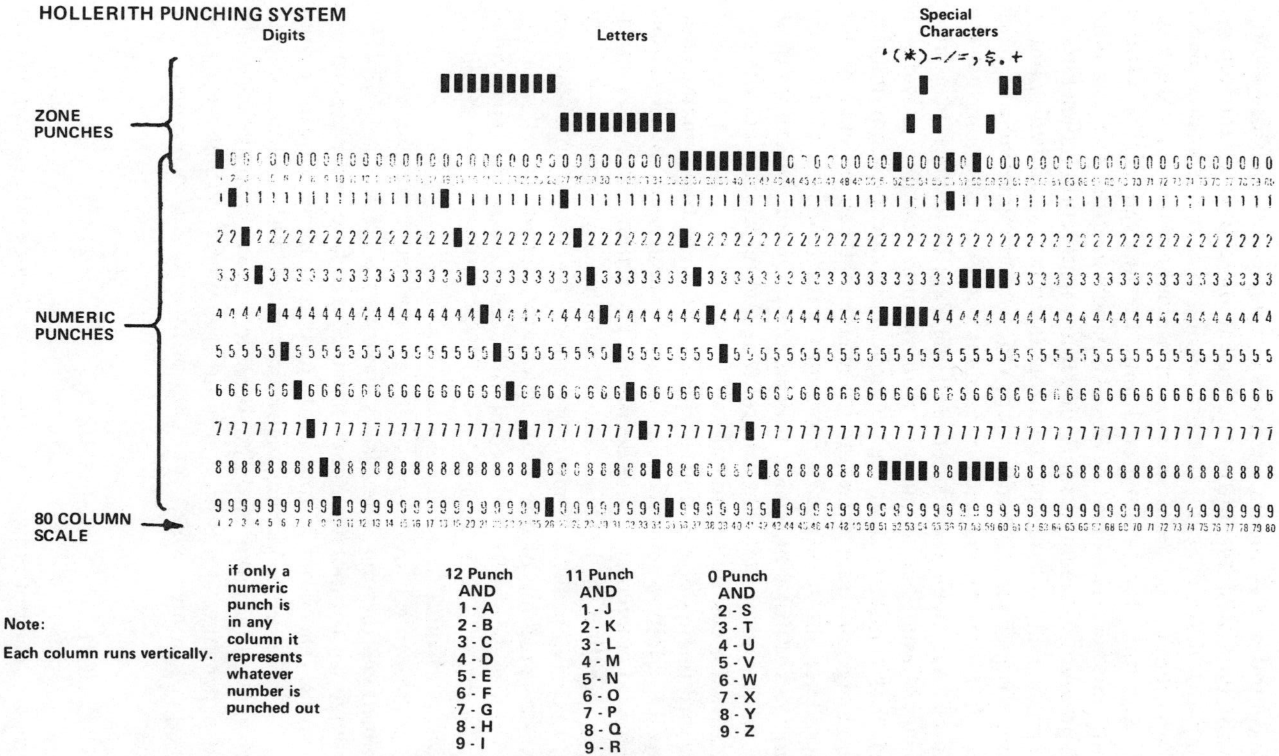

HOLLERITH PUNCHING SYSTEM

Digits

Letters

Special Characters

ZONE PUNCHES

NUMERIC PUNCHES

80 COLUMN SCALE

Each column runs vertically.

Note:
if only a numeric punch is in any column it represents whatever number is punched out

12 Punch	11 Punch	0 Punch
AND	AND	AND
1 - A	1 - J	2 - S
2 - B	2 - K	3 - T
3 - C	3 - L	4 - U
4 - D	4 - M	5 - V
5 - E	5 - N	6 - W
6 - F	6 - O	7 - X
7 - G	7 - P	8 - Y
8 - H	8 - Q	9 - Z
9 - I	9 - R	

Figure 2–1. Punched card medium (Source: Tomeski, Edward A. *The Computer Revolution*. London: Macmillan, 1970 [p. 141])

19

The central processing unit consists of three parts: the storage unit, the control unit, and the arithmetic-logical unit. It is in the central processing unit that the actual data processing and analysis takes place. First, the computer program, written in a symbolic language such as Fortran, and the data are entered into the storage of the central processing unit via some input device like punched cards. The computer tests the program instructions for errors. If any instruction is illegitimate, the computer will not accept the program but instead will print a diagnostic—a question of clarification. Once the programming instructions are all legitimate, the deck of cards is compiled, showing that the instructions have been understood and the data have been translated into binary form. The computer manufacturer usually provides a compiler that translates a given symbolic language program into an object language program (machine language) that can be used by the computer. Then the sequence of program instructions is carried out by action in the control unit, which triggers the required computations in the arithmetic-logical unit. The control unit also terminates activities as indicated by the computer program.

The arithmetic-logical unit performs the four basic mathematic functions of addition, subtraction, multiplication, and division, plus making logical comparisons and decisions. The arithmetic-logical unit is similar in operation to the desk calculator in that accumulators in both are used to carry out the arithmetic operations. By comparison, however, the physical position of the desk calculator accumulators indicates values, whereas the values in the computer accumulators are represented by the location of magnetic charges. The difference in speed of operations is obvious.

Once the central processing unit has completed the processing of programmed instructions, the results have to be made available. The medium used for computer output will vary according to the desired use of the results. The input/output medium that is most frequently used because of its speed is the magnetic tape drive. Other output device alternatives parallel input medium: console typewriter, punched cards, punched paper tape, and cathode-ray tube. A special output medium is the high speed printer, which produces printed results to the user.

INTRODUCTION TO PROGRAMMING

Managers are not required to become sophisticated programmers in order to make use of the computer as a decision-making tool; however, a manager should understand the basic fundamentals of programming.

Space does not permit description of programming in this text; rather the reader can find numerous texts on the subject. The manager is expected to understand how to provide data and access into a computer in the utilization of prepared programs described below. An illustrative example is presented.

PREPARED PROGRAMS

A large number of prepared programs are available to the business decision maker who wishes to utilize the computer but who does not want to become a programming specialist. Computer manufacturers provide manuals that contain numerous examples of prepared programs. By supplying appropriate instruction cards, a manager can obtain a computer analysis of a problem with the aid of a prepared program. For example, only eight instructions are needed to supplement the BIMD 02R prepared program for running a stepwise regression solution (technique is described in a later chapter) on a Control Data computer. These instructions are presented in Figure 2-2.

Card #1—Job order card. Starting with column 31, punch your name.
       Write BIMD 02R on front of card.

Card #2—Problem card.
       In columns 1–6, punch PROBLM.
       In columns 10–15, punch REGRES.
       In columns 17–20, punch the number of data cards, one for each line of data, to be read by the computer, for example, 0030.
       In columns 24, 25, punch the number of variables (including dependent variable), for example, 04.
       In columns 29, 30, punch 00.
       In columns 34, 35, punch 00.
       In columns 44, 45, punch 01.
       In columns 59–61, punch YES.
       In columns 71, 72, punch 01.

Card #3—In column 1, punch % key—this will appear as parenthesis left symbol.
       In columns 2, 3, punch the number of variables (including the dependent variable), for example, 04.
       In column 4, punch F.
       In column 5, punch the number of digits in the longest data field, for example, 7 for million values plus any fields to be allowed for decimal places.

In column 6, punch a decimal point.

In column 7, punch the number of decimal fields to be used in data.

In column 8, punch □ key which will appear as parenthesis right symbol.

All data values must be punched with the same number of digit fields and the same number of decimal fields. This might involve using zeros preceding a value and also following a decimal point.

Card #4—Data deck of cards. Starting with column 1, on first data card, punch first value of the dependent variable with the number of digits and number or decimal fields as defined in card #3. Without skipping a column, type the values of each independent variable, related to the first dependent variable value, with the same length of digit and decimal fields.

Follow the same procedure on other data cards for each dependent variable values and related independent variable values. (You should have a card for each row of values in your problem.)

Card #5—In columns 1–6, punch SVBPRO.

In columns 9, 10, punch 01.

In columns 49, 50, punch 01.

In columns 63–65, punch YES.

Card #6—In columns 1–6, punch IDXPLT.

In columns 7, 8, punch 01.

Card #7—In columns 1–6, punch FINISH.

Card #8—In columns 1–4, punch *END.

Figure 2–2. Computer program instructions for running stepwise multiple-regression problems on CDC6400

Management science specialists in industry and at universities have developed numerous prepared programs. There is a distinct need to have a comprehensive information dispersal of the available programs. The specialists have organized national organizations like the American Institute of Decision Sciences and the Operations Research Society of America. Information is exchanged at meetings and in journals. There is an excellent monthly publication called *Computing Newsletter*, edited by J. Daniel Couger of the University of Colorado, which reports the latest happenings in computer developments.

Personnel at other institutions have initiated publications to inform decision makers of available programs. One example is the group in the Department of Quantitative Methods at Georgia State University, which publishes a periodic newsletter. The following items appeared in a recent issue:

The manual *Time-Sharing System Applications in the De-cision Sciences*, which provides an introduction to the time-sharing system at Georgia State and instructions for the most frequently used time-sharing programs, has been revised and updated. Improvements and corrections have been made in both the basic terminal instructions and the programs.

Four new analyses of variance programs have been added—STAT13, STAT14, STAT15, and DUNONE, along with an improved and more comprehensive multiple-regression program—MULFIT9. SEASALL, another new addition, allows the user three alternative methods of calculating seasonal variation, and a much improved version of DYSLP, entitled GSULP, has been developed. The new LP program is more accurate and readable than previous programs.

Professor Bert Greynolds has developed five programs for *Time-Sharing System Applications in Accounting* and these have been included in this manual. His program, PVCALL, calculates present values; INTRAATE calculates internal rate of return; PLOT5 plots data points; PLOTTO5 plots two functions; and SIMEQM solves linear equations.[3]

The Data and Program Library Service for the Social Sciences (DPLS) of the University of Wisconsin has undertaken to develop a national index to computer programs. This agency has been drawing up a comprehensive inventory of program resources and has been distributing this inventory in the form of indexes and abstracts. The index has entries showing the coding system explanation for abstracts in key word and author index, file number index, and address addendum for the complete addresses of program sources.

It would seem that a manager has access to many prepared computer programs to assist him in applying mathematical models in the decision-making process. There is no need for him to become an expert programmer in order to benefit from computer operations. An ideal arrangement is for a manager to be supplied with a time-sharing remote terminal through which he can call for various prepared programs. The program data could then be entered into the computer operations and a printout of results produced in a very short period of time. The decision-making effectiveness should be enhanced greatly as a result of the increased use of prepared computer programs in the analytical stage of problem solving.

[3] Time sharing system applications in the decision sciences is revised. *Decision Sciences at Georgia State*, 1(1972): 6.

CHAPTER 3

Development of Computer Applications in Decision Making

Managers in the past have abdicated responsibility in designing computer systems to assist them in the decision-making process. The typical manager did not have sufficient knowledge to contribute to the systems development. Technical computer analysts, on the other hand, who did develop computer systems, did not understand all of the complexities involved in decision making, especially the subjectivities that were involved. The managers also had natural distrust of any computer systems that they did not completely understand; many agreed with Robert Townsend's conclusion in *Up the Organization* that "The computer technicians are building a mystique. . .to keep you from knowing what they are doing." Consequently, early computer systems did not significantly enhance the decision-making process. The computer has been available, but management has failed to use it to change and improve its decision-making processes.[1]

A computer is not a panacea to problem solving; rather it is an effective method of investigating a problem. Such computer application requires cooperation between the manager and computer analyst. No longer is the process merely one in which the manager describes a problem to a computer analyst who then develops a model that provides a solution. Instead, the two must work together, the manager providing insights into the problem situation so that the analyst can recognize the full complexities of the problem and the analyst providing the technical expertise of computer application. An example of this cooperation is as follows:

> One company involved in a wide range of manufacturing
> activities requiring a high level of technology had developed a

---

[1] Neuschel, Robert P. Unleashing computer power. *Business Horizons,* 14(February, 1971): 82.

new type of packaging equipment. This equipment was particularly oriented to food packaging, but was adaptable to other types of household commodities as well. A considerable investment in engineering effort had been made to produce an operating prototype. While some questions remained as to an appropriate market entry strategy, three conclusions had been tentatively agreed to by top management:

1. Since considerable investment had already been made, management did not want to extend its investment much further. Therefore, if the project was not operating at a gross profit at the end of one year, it would be dropped.

2. The major market opportunity was believed to be a single end-user segment, for which the prototype had been built. No modification of this prototype for other end-user segments would be necessary or worth the additional investment.

3. Also because of the concentration of the end-user market, the marketing group could pick up this product as a part of the existing product line. No additional marketing staff would be required.

To check the validity of these tentative conclusions, a risk-analysis model of the financial implications of the project was built. Risk analysis was chosen because the number of possible results in the marketplace was quite large, even though the eventual profitability of the project was felt to be secure. Because of their lack of confidence in projecting market performance, management was willing to make projections only in terms of ranges of possible outcomes, not single point estimates. Consequently, the risk analysis format, projecting the full range of possible outcomes and weighing the relative likelihood of each, was ideal.

The president of this company supplied the data. He spent the better part of a day with a knowledgeable analyst discussing the project—likely costs to be incurred, selling price, machine performance, and so forth. He also responded to the criterion that detail must be determined by importance, and quickly summarized the bulk of the production data and got to the core of the problem: likely market performance. The total market was broken into end-user segments, and each segment was evaluated as to total potential, likely conversion rates to the new packaging machine, timing, and the share of the market this company could expect. For each of these factors, the full range of possible results, as well as their relative likelihood, was assessed. Of some 500 bits of data collected—not large by data processing standards—over 75 percent were aimed at describing the market.

Time-shared computing was selected to provide the shortest possible development time and to provide flexibility in additional analysis which was expected. The analyst required less than a day to develop and program the model, enter the data, and conduct the initial analysis. The following morning the president was presented with these conclusions from the model:

Management's overall optimism about the success of the project was warranted; there was a better than 95 percent chance for the success of the project over a five-year period. However, there was a 90 percent chance of loss during the first year, and no reliable relationship between first-year performance and the ultimate success of the project. Management's first criteria for evaluating the project at the end of one year should be changed.

The largest single market segment was one that could not be served by the machine which had been developed. Entering this segment would require substantial modification of the prototype. The engineering effort needed to do this should be invested immediately to assure the success of the project. Competitive equipment was already being produced to serve this market, and an important opportunity could be lost if the company failed to move quickly.

Moreover, no single end-user segment offered a substantial enough opportunity to assure the success of the total project. Additional marketing support would be required to exploit the full range of opportunities.

Since the conclusions suggested by the risk analysis model represented rather important differences from the tentative conclusions that management had accepted earlier, the president was naturally concerned. He wanted some redundance to check out these conclusions. He consulted individually with his vice-president, development, and vice-president, marketing, getting their estimates of each of the input data. The model was rerun with the new data. While there were individual differences in some of the market performance estimates, the conclusions suggested by the model remained unchanged.

A meeting of the top management group was then called

to iron out individual differences in estimated performance and to reach agreement on a new direction for the project. Here the conversational characteristic of time-sharing proved vital in assisting the management interchanges. Various assumptions were tested, and a sensitivity analysis was run during the course of this meeting. Turnaround times of more than five minutes would have been too long. The time-share computer effectively entered the conversation with management relying on a limited but efficiently constructed data base to assist management in strategic decision making."[2]

The preceding example shows clearly the role of the manager in the development of computer analysis of a problem. The vital data to be analyzed were supplied by the manager, whereas the computer analyst developed the model to be used.

One significant benefit of the manager-analyst cooperation in developing computer applications is the clearer understanding that the manager achieves in the process. The manager must verbalize the decision model that would assist him in solving a particular problem. A diagram, Figure 3–1, may be used to illustrate the cooperative process.

Another significant benefit derived from the manager-analyst cooperation in developing computer applications is the determination of what information is to be collected. It has been stated that "The most critical question involved in designing a management information system is the determination of what information is necessary to enable the manager to effectively make decisions."[3] As the manager explains the problem situation, the analyst can obtain a better understanding of the data required for developing a computer model to assist in the decision-making process. The model may be used at any one of four various phases in the decision process as shown in Figure 3–2. The phase in which the manager is seeking assistance will determine the type of data that is necessary. The four phases are elaborated as follows:

1. A computer information system may simply provide data about a problem to the manager.
2. A computer information system may be used to supply predictions concerning alternative actions.
3. A sophisticated mathematical model may be used to provide an

---

[2] Plummer, John. A human model for computer systems. *Business Horizons,* 14(April, 1971): 40–41.

[3] King, William R., and Cleland, David I. Manager-analyst teamwork in MIS. *Business Horizons,* 14(April, 1971): 63.

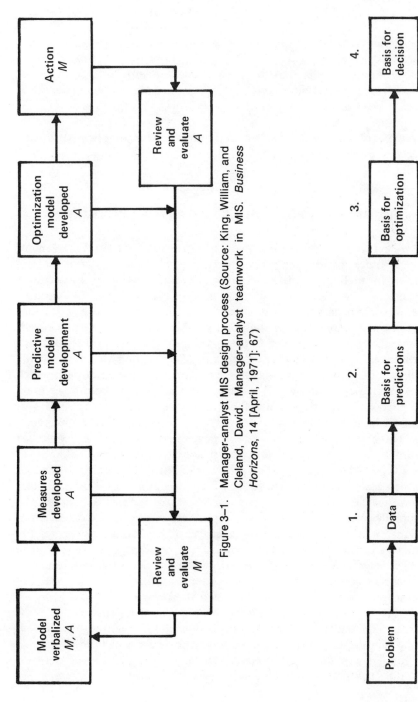

Figure 3–1. Manager-analyst MIS design process (Source: King, William, and Cleland, David. Manager-analyst teamwork in MIS. *Business Horizons*, 14 [April, 1971]: 67)

Figure 3–2.

29

optimum solution to a problem situation for management consideration.
4. A computer model may be programmed to provide a decision for action in problem situations of a routine nature, for example, stock reorders in an inventory control model.

The type of data required becomes increasingly complicated as one proceeds from Phase 1 to Phase 4.

MANAGEMENT EVALUATION OF COMPUTER OPERATIONS

A computer installation should be considered a capital investment as are other major equipment purchases. Evaluation of a capital investment includes the fixed expense of the purchase price spread over the life of the equipment (or the leasing charge) plus the variable operating expenses. The ideal criterion for determining computer capacity is to expand up to the point at which marginal revenue equals marginal cost. In any operation the optimum point stated is very difficult to discover. It is even more difficult in the case of computers because the equipment is still new and management lacks the experience with which to calculate payoff amounts. Cost-benefit analyses will also differ among companies in the way in which the computer is utilized, so management must evaluate their own situation as a particular set of circumstances.

Three possible alternatives for charging for the use of computer facilities within an organization are (1) nonchargeout, (2) full chargeout, and (3) partial chargeout. Each system has possible benefits, depending on the specific company situation. Figure 3-3 shows a listing of factors to consider in analyzing each of the charging systems. Generally the companies that use the computer installation for standardized applications, which are highly centralized, and that do not have readily available outside services tend toward the nonchargeout system. The companies with diverse applications, which are decentralized, and that have ready access to outside services tend toward the partial and full chargeout systems. One study indicated that:

> The full chargeout system is the control system toward which most companies should work. For the present, however, until companies gain experience in controlling the resources, full chargeout will cause many problems, and most companies

would be well advised to adopt partial chargeout systems fitted
to their particular stage of computer development.[4]

Planned Program for Computer Utilization

One means for increasing the benefits from computer utilization is
to design a planned program of operations. Robert P. Neuschel presents
the following actions:[5]

1. "Identify high pay-out applications." Objective is to assign high
   priorities for computer utilization on important profit-bearing opportunities.
2. "Select a balanced 'menu' of computer applications." Objective is to
   balance the number of projects undertaken with the size of the
   computer staff available and to balance low- and moderate-risk
   projects along with one or two high-risk applications.
3. "Increase involvement by key line management." Objective is to
   involve line managers in both the identification and selection of
   projects. Two approaches are suggested: (1) assign at least one key
   manager with experience in each of the major functions of the
   business to the computer staff or (2) use project teams staffed by
   temporary transfers from operating departments.
4. "Subject applications to rigorous preevaluation." Objective is to select
   computer projects that will maximize profit by being technically
   feasible, have greatest economic returns, and can be put into
   operation.
5. "Cultivate tough realism on what can be done and how soon."
   Objective is to establish strong credibility and confidence between
   management and the computer analysts in the capability of the
   computer system.
6. "Bring the computer and decision maker together." Objective is to
   help managers make better decisions by understanding the power and
   limitations of the computer.

It is believed that management can increase the payoff from
computer utilization by following a carefully designed program of
operations.

---

[4] Dearden, John, and Nolan, Richard L. How to control the computer resource. *Harvard Business Review,* 51(November, 1973): 76.

[5] Neuschel, Robert P. Unleashing computer power. *Business Horizons,* 14(February, 1971): 83–86.

Managerial awareness	Spectrum		
	Non-chargeout	Partial chargeout	Full chargeout
1. Are the major opportunities for computer applications known and understood by users and management?	No	⟷	Yes
2. Are users knowledgeable about the costs and limitations of computers?	No	⟷	Yes
3. Are users highly susceptible to "overselling" of the computer resource?	Yes	⟷	No
4. Alternatively, are their needs diverse—for example, for graphics, mathematical modeling, and routine accounting work?	No	⟷	Yes

Organizational issues	Spectrum		
	Non-chargeout	Partial chargeout	Full chargeout
1. Is the company's operating philosophy one of centralization? If so, do the management control system and the location of the resource reflect this fact?	Yes	⟷	No
2. Is the company's operating philosophy one of decentralization? If so, do the management control system and the location of the resource reflect this fact?	No	⟷	Yes
3. Do users require very highly advanced technology (for example, for graphics, on-line data entry, software) with an extended time horizon?	Yes	⟷	No

5. Do most potential users have standardized needs?

Yes ⟵——————⟶ No

4. Can they justify these requirements on the basis of company strategy?

No ⟵——————⟶ Yes

5. Does security dictate that many data and programs be processed in-house?

Yes ⟵——————⟶ No

Management issues

1. Do complex priorities make it difficult to generate needed management information on schedule?

No ⟵——————⟶ Yes

2. Are outside services readily available?

No ⟵——————⟶ Yes

3. Is it necessary to monitor and control EDP management closely?

No ⟵——————⟶ Yes

Figure 3–3. Analysis of nonchargeant/chargeant decisions (Source: Dearden, John, and Nolan, Richard L. How to control the computer resource. *Harvard Business Review*, 51 [November, 1973]: 78)

Management Audit of Computer Operations[6]

A specific tool by which management can evaluate the accomplishments of computer operations is a regular audit (every two or three years) augmented by a progress review committee. The top executive should probably be assigned responsibility for the audit and also should be a member of the progress review committee. The management audit should have as its purpose the appraisal of computer activities in terms of accomplishments, present status, effectiveness, cost and benefits, and future business needs. Hollinger indicates that computer activities can be classified into five major areas: planning, systems applications, operations and control, organization, and standards and documentation. An effective management audit should examine each of these areas.

Planning is a key area for auditing. Current activity and future plans constitute the two areas in which potential computer contribution to profit is greatest. It is estimated that two out of three companies need to improve in the area of applications planning. The audit should evaluate plans where they exist and review them in light of business needs. Of course, if plans do not exist, the audit should make provisions for them.

Systems application, the second area of the audit investigation, concerns the use of computer facilities to meet the needs of the company. Those in the company who use computer printout reports can be very helpful to the auditors in evaluating systems applications. They can report on the degree of usefulness of various printouts, leading to the possible elimination or reduced frequency of some. Interviews of users will also indicate how well they understand the reports and whether the reports are being used in the most effective manner. This step in the audit may lead to significant improvements in the usefulness of the computer data production.

Another aspect of the audit is an analysis of computer operations and control. Following are typical questions that should be considered:

> Are present operating control practices satisfactory?
>
> Are operating expenses measured and controlled effectively?
>
> What has been the trend of costs and how do these costs compare with services provided?
>
> Is efficient utilization of regular and overtime machine hours being obtained?
>
> Are present procedures for reporting utilization and scheduling equipment adequate?

---

[6] Factual information is taken from Hollinger, Robert C. Managing the computer for competitive advantage. *Business Horizons*, 13(December, 1970): 18.

Is computer capacity consistent with current and near-term needs?

How do expenses in total compare with other companies of equivalent size and scope?

What equipment should be owned, rented, or leased through a third-party arrangement to minimize annual computer costs.[7]

Audit of where the computer system is located within a business's organization should indicate whether the facility is being managed in an effective manner. The accepted practice has been to place authority over the computer facility in the business operation which will use the service most. Therefore it is not surprising that in many instances the controller had authority over the computer system, since early use of the computer lay in accounting applications. As computer operations expanded to service other departments, the jurisdiction of authority changed. The trend is toward placing computer operations under the responsibility of a top executive whose primary responsibility is corporate management information systems.

The last recommended area for audit is the area of standards and documentation. An efficient computer operation requires accurate documentation of all systems applications. A major weakness in many installations is the lack of adequate systems documentation presented in a standard form that is easily understood. It is obvious that computer operations will be less than efficient if procedures are not clearly presented and understood by the computer staff and users.

A progress review committee should be established to review implementation of the management audit. This committee should maintain a monthly progress review chart as the one illustrated in Figure 3–4. Benefits of the progress review are as follows:

1. It provides both management and the computer organization with a clear understanding of what is expected from the company's computer effort and when these results should occur.
2. It provides management with a means of readily evaluating the accomplishments of its computer efforts.
3. It identifies where management attention is needed to obtain the systems benefits.[8]

It is through this management committee that a company can determine the progress being made toward implementation of the long-range plans outlined in the management audit.

---

[7] *Ibid.*, p. 22.
[8] *Ibid.*, p. 28.

Monthly Periods

Savings Category		1	2	3	4	5	6	7	8	9	10	11	12
Keypunching staff	Planned		1,000	1,000	1,000	1,000	1,000	1,000	1,000	1,000	1,000	1,000	1,000
	Actual												
Billing staff	Planned						3,000	3,000	3,000	3,000	3,000	3,000	3,000
	Actual												
Accounts receivable staff	Planned										4,400	4,400	4,400
	Actual												
Equipment rental	Planned		4,200	4,200	4,200	8,600	8,600	8,600	8,600	8,600	8,600	8,600	8,600
	Actual												
Inventory carrying cost	Planned												
	Actual												
Total monthly savings	Planned		5,200	5,200	5,200	9,600	12,600	12,600	12,600	12,600	17,000	17,000	17,000
	Actual												
Cumulative savings	Planned		5,200	10,400	15,600	25,200	37,800	50,400	63,000	75,600	92,600	109,600	126,600
	Actual												
Cumulative development costs	Planned	3,000	8,000	14,000	20,000	26,000	32,000	40,000	50,000	60,000	70,000	80,000	86,000
	Actual												

Figure 3–4. Progress review chart (Source: Hollinger, Robert C. Managing the computer for competitive advantage. *Business Horizons*, 13 [December, 1970]: 27)

36

Time-Sharing Operations

Time sharing is a situation in which users at many locations can simultaneously utilize a remote computer by means of a telephone line. An individual user can dial the telephone number of two time-sharing services and have immediate contact with a multimillion dollar computer that has been comprehensively programmed to solve a wide range of problems. Growth of time-sharing service has been estimated to be from $10 million in 1965 to $1 billion in 1975.[9]

Time-sharing operations can be beneficial to all sizes of companies, ranging from small and medium sized to the large sized. A large-sized company can enjoy the benefits of a time-sharing facility completely contained within its own operation. A company that is too small to support its own computer service can contract with an independent time-sharing service. The company can thus improve its competitive position, obtain continuous updating of the data files, have better protection of records than it could afford, reduce clerical needs, and improve customer service.

A medium-sized company, which could support its own computer facilities, can instead realize distinct benefits from utilizing time-sharing services too. There is less need for specialized computer personnel in the company to do programming and computer management. Less space is needed for time-sharing facilities than for in-house computer operations. Time-sharing performance is more efficient than batch processing in which a user must submit punched cards and wait his turn for computer time. If there is a programming error, the user in batch processing must start the waiting process all over again. Time-sharing operations offer instantaneous interaction in which the user appears to be receiving immediate attention.

Possible hazards in the utilization of independent time-sharing operations should be considered. Various services differ in hardware applications, programming, technical capability, and financial backing. Inadequacy in any one of these could cause service interruptions, logjams, or loss of data. There is also the danger of illicit tapping of private data files. Generally, however, these hazards can be avoided with proper planning and control.

Examples of Time-Sharing Operations

Statistical analysis. Dow Chemical Company is making extensive use of time-sharing operations with about 150 terminals in research

---

[9] CPA's evaluation of the business computer utility. *Journal of Accounting*, 131(March, 1971): 51.

laboratories and production areas within the organization.[10] Routine applications include statistical analysis in production control and forecasting. The company is equipped with an IBM System/370 Model 155 and a large library of advanced computer programs. These programs are designed to solve many types of problems. A representative of Dow believes that time-sharing operations have helped greatly to put computational capability into the hands of engineers and scientists. As a result, these technical people have increased their job productivity.

Financial forecasting. First National City Bank has developed a time-sharing system that provides a tool for divisional or corporate forecasting, planning, and acquisition analysis. The system is designed to accomplish the detail computations in forecasting and planning, enabling the manager to concentrate his efforts on making decisions based on the computer printout.

The system is called COMMAND (COMputer-assisted MANagement Decisions) and is described as follows:

> Conceptually, COMMAND is an automated accounting framework of any company division or plant. It can best be visualized as a computerized columnar pad. On the left side of the pad is a list of all the accounting nomenclature that is used in a company's financial statements and analytical reports. Across the pad there is provision for up to 12 months, 12 quarters, or 12 years of figures.
>
> The figures for the 12 blank periods are generated from a series of assumptions developed by the financial manager for each accounting item listed. For example, the financial manager assumes that sales will increase by 10 percent for each of the next five years. The computer will apply a 10 percent compound growth rate to sales and generate a dollar sales forecast.
>
> Accomplishment of this task requires only that a case "1" (meaning fixed growth rate) and the entry "10" be made onto a worksheet next to the line marked "Sales." Similar assumptions are entered onto the worksheet for each component of the income statement, balance sheet, and cash-flow statement. Each accounting category can be forecast by applying a fixed growth rate for all periods, a different growth rate for each period, a percentage of some related variable, or a dollar amount. In addition, a number of different statistical forecasting techniques are available within the system.

---

[10] At Dow Chemical, a tradition of growth. *Computing Report,* 9(Spring, 1973): 3.

Once all of the assumptions have been developed, they are typed from the worksheet into a computer terminal at the financial manager's desk. They flow across a standard telephone line into a local time-shared computer. In minutes, all calculations are made and a complete set of forecasted statements are printed at the terminal on the financial executive's desk.

Experience has shown that the best forecasts are those based upon the input of the company's financial manager, not statistical extrapolations. The forecast will only be as good as the "computer" on the financial manager's shoulders. His knowledge and assumptions are the most important ingredients in the forecasting process. Now, however, instead of pushing a pencil and living uncomfortably with one manual forecast, he can devote his time to analyzing, thinking about alternative courses of action, and making decisions.[11]

Mathematical models. Many companies, both large and small, are utilizing computers in the application of mathematical models to decision making. One reference indicated that there were 50 successful management science applications listed in a casebook of applications used by management consultants in 1968–1969 compared to only two listed in 1960–1961.[12] These models include such techniques as simulation, linear programming, and heuristics, all of which are explained in full detail in later chapters.

To cite one example of mathematical model application:

Plant expansion alternatives are analyzed with a linear programming model at the Joseph Schlitz Brewing Company in Milwaukee, Wisconsin. The program enables Schlitz executives to examine operating costs as a function of consumer demand and production capacity. Such a model has to be relatively accurate since variations of only one-tenth of a percent in operating costs could represent $500,000, a significant amount relative to an investment of $7 to $8 million. Use of the model shows not only cash flows from a particular investment, but also the gains and losses to be expected from building a series of plants at different times.[13]

---

[11] Druger, Leonard N. Computer time-sharing aids in forecasting. *Financial Executive,* 40(August, 1972): 20, 21.

[12] The management sciences are ready for business. *Computer Decisions,* 46(January, 1972): 32.

[13] *Ibid.,* p. 33.

CHAPTER 4

Bayesian Decision Making

INTRODUCTION

The decision maker, when applying the theory of traditional classical statistics, generally will design a problem-solving procedure based on a test in which a hypothesis is established and then he will either accept it or reject it. For example, a machine tool originally set to produce only 2 percent defectives may be examined for precision of output. The hypothesis—that the machine is still performing according to the desired setup—can be tested at a predetermined level of significance. Sample data are collected and the hypothesis is accepted if the sample results fall within the test limits and rejected if the sample results fall outside of the test limits.

The typical statistics textbook shows the test of hypothesis distribution in the form of a normal curve with reference points: (1) hypothesis value as the mean value, (2) a value equal to the mean plus two standard deviations, and (3) a value equal to the mean minus two standard deviations.

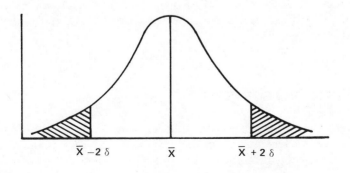

$$\overline{X} - 2\,\delta \qquad \overline{X} \qquad \overline{X} + 2\,\delta$$

41

The range of values between $\bar{x} \pm 2\sigma$ represents the acceptance range of 95.44 percent and the values above and below the range of $\bar{x} \pm 2\sigma$ represent the rejection limits. According to statistical theory the decision maker who utilizes the above test design will accept the hypothesis, and it will be a correct decision, 95.44 percent of the time and will reject it, when it is true, 4.56 percent of the time (Type I error). The decision-making procedure can also be illustrated in a decision matrix as follows:

	State of Nature	
	S_1: True	S_2: False
A_1: Accept hypothesis	Correct hypothesis	Incorrect hypothesis
A_2: Reject hypothesis	Incorrect decision	Correct decision

The probabilities of success are controlled by the decision maker according to the acceptance range that he establishes. Instead of using $\bar{x} \pm 2\sigma$, the decision maker may utilize any fraction of standard deviation in determining the probabilities of acceptance or rejection. Most commonly the range of $\bar{x} \pm 1.96\sigma$ is employed, providing a test situation in which the decision maker will accept the hypothesis, and it will be a correct decision, 95 percent of the time.

Using the classical approach for the illustrative example, the decision maker observes a sample of machine output and decides to accept or reject the hypothesis that the machine is still performing according to the desired setup. However, there is no basis for determining the *probability* that the hypothesis (state of nature) is true. In the statistical framework using Bayesian analysis, inferences are made about the probability of a state of nature. In other words, given a certain observed action, what is the probability of a certain state of nature? Using the Bayesian approach for the illustrative example, a decision maker could assign probability values to the hypothesis that the machine is still performing according to the desired setup. Then he could compute the expected cost (in the form of defectives) of continuing the present machine operations versus the expected cost of machine shutdown for readjustment purposes.

ELEMENTS OF PROBABILITY

Before examining Bayesian statistics in detail, it would be beneficial to study the elements of probability that are incorporated in the Bayesian concept. Probability is based on the notion of set theory.

Set Theory

The term "set" in mathematics is an undefined term, just as "line" and "point" are. A *set* can be considered to be a collection or class of "things" called *elements*. All the elements in a set need not be alike. For example, a set can consist of all the planets in the universe and all the professional football players in the United States. In order for a collection of things to form a set, the collection must be well defined to the extent that it is possible to determine whether or not a particular object belongs to the set.

Sets will be denoted by capital letters. Lower case letters will denote elements of a set. If a is an element of set S, we say $a \in S$. If a is not in S, we write $a \notin S$. Sets can contain no elements, a finite number of elements, or an infinite number of elements. The set that contains no elements is called the *null* or *empty set* and is designated by ϕ.

Sets can be completely described by two methods. If the set membership is small, all the elements can be listed, the names of the elements being enclosed in braces { }. For example, the set containing the first five positive integers would be $S = \{1, 2, 3, 4, 5\}$. Each element of a set is listed just once, and the order in which the elements are listed is immaterial.

Example 4.1   The ages of the partners of a corporation are given below.

Jones	65 years
Johnson	31 years
Jason	57 years
Jenkins	31 years

If S is the set, the elements of which are the ages of the partners, then

$$S = \{65, 31, 57\}$$

completely describes the set.

If all the elements of a set have a common property that is the basis for set membership, then the "set-builder" notation can be used.

Example 4.2   If S is the set of positive integers, then in set-builder notation

$$S = \{x \mid x \in \text{integers}, x > 0\}$$

which is read S is the set of elements x such that x is an integer and x is greater than zero. Thus S is an example of a set that contains an infinite number of elements.

The term *subset* is used to describe a collection of part of a set. A set A is a subset of another set B if every element in A is also in B, denoted by $A \subseteq B$. The notation $A \subset B$ indicates that there is at least one element in B that is not in A, or A is a *proper* subset of B. Two sets A and B are equal if each is a subset of the other. The empty set is considered to be a subset of every set.

Example 4.3   Let

$$A = \{1, 2, 3\}$$
$$B = \{1, 2, 3, 4, 5\}$$
$$C = \{5, 4, 1, 2, 3\}$$

Then $A \subset B$, $A \subset C$, $B \subseteq C$, and $B = C$, $C \subseteq B$.

Example 4.4   Let

$$S = \{1, 2\}$$

All the subsets of S are ϕ, $\{1\}$, $\{2\}$, $\{1, 2\}$.

The *universal* set $\mathcal{U}$ is the set that contains all the elements under consideration in a particular situation or discussion.

Let A and B be subsets of a universal set. The *union* of A and B, designated $A \cup B$, is the set of all elements of $\mathcal{U}$ that belong to either A or B or both. In set-builder notation

$$A \cup B = \{x \mid x \in A \text{ or } x \in B, \text{ or both}\}$$

The *intersection* of A and B, designated $A \cap B$, is the set of all elements of $\mathcal{U}$ that belong to both A and B.

$$A \cap B = \{ x \mid x \in A \text{ and } x \in B \}$$

The *complement* of a set A is the set, designated A', that has as its members elements which belong to $\mathcal{U}$, but do not belong to A.

$$A' = \{ x \mid x \in \mathcal{U} \; x \notin A \}$$

Two sets A and B are said to be *disjoint* if they have no elements in common or, equivalently, if $A \cap B = \phi$.

Example 4.5 $\mathcal{U} = \{1, 2, 3, 4, 5, 6, 7, 8, 9, 10\}$

$$A = \{1, 2, 3\} \qquad B = \{3, 4, 5\} \qquad C = \{9, 10\}$$

$A \cup B$	$= \{ 1, 2, 3, 4, 5 \}$	ϕ'	$= \mathcal{U}$
$A \cap B$	$= \{ 3 \}$	$\mathcal{U}'$	$= \phi$
$A \cup C$	$= \{ 1, 2, 3, 9, 10 \}$	$\phi \cup \mathcal{U}$	$= 1, 2, 3, 4, 5, 6, 7, 8, 9, 10$
$A \cap B$	$= \phi$	$\phi \cap \mathcal{U}$	$= \phi$
A'	$= \{ 4, 5, 6, 7, 8, 9, 10 \}$	C'	$= 1, 2, 3, 4, 5, 6, 7, 8$
$A' \cap C'$	$= \{ 4, 5, 6, 7, 8 \}$	$A \cap B \cap C$	$= \phi$

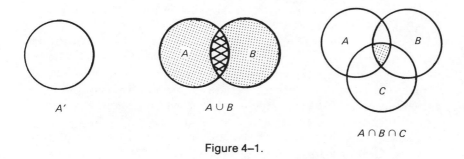

Figure 4–1.

Venn diagrams are used to visualize complements, intersections, and unions of sets. In Figure 4–1 the rectangle represents the universal set $\mathscr{U}$, the circle or circles represent subsets of $\mathscr{U}$. The points within the circles represent elements of sets; the points in the rectangle, but outside the circles, represent points in the universal set but not in the sets represented by the circles. If A, B, and C are subsets of $\mathscr{U}$, then unions, intersections, and complements can be represented by shading appropriate regions of the Venn diagram.

Probability Axioms

Basis for the manipulation of probabilities are three axioms.

1. The probability that an event will occur is a number between 0 and 1 as follows:

$$0 \le P(E) \le 1$$

2. Given a set of all possible events, the probability is 1 that one of these events will occur:

$$P(S) = 1$$

3. Given two events, the occurrence of one precluding the occurrence of the other (they are then said to be mutually exclusive), the probability that either one or the other will occur is equal to the total of their probabilities:

$$P(E \text{ or } F) = P(E) + P(F)$$

The same proposition applies to any number of events.

In the first proposition, the extreme possibilities of the occurrence of an event range from no chance, or $P = 0$, to certainty which is $P = 1$. Different degrees of uncertainty are expressed in intermediate values between 0 and 1. A value outside of the range of 0 to 1 has no relevance to the theory of probability.

In the second proposition, if all possible events are included in a trial (a universal set), the probability that one event of the set will occur, that is, $P(S) = 1$, is a truism. It is the decision maker's responsibility to include all possible solution alternatives within his considerations, thereby insuring that one of the considered alternatives must occur.

In the third proposition, if events are mutually exclusive, the probability that the events will occur equals the total of their probabilities. Total probability of all possible events is 1.0. A decision maker can total the probabilities of all events in his analysis in order to determine if the probability of events being considered equals 1.0. If the total probability is less than 1.0, then he knows that the analysis is incomplete.

Computations of Probabilities

Development of Bayesian statistics involves computations of probabilities. The different elements of probabilities included in the computations are prior probability, conditional probability, joint probability, and posterior probability. Prior probability is a chance-occurrence estimate based on empirical data, that is, $P(E)$. In the example of rolling two "fair" dice, prior probability is stated thus: What is the probability of having the dice come up with a total equal to 7 or more? The answer is 21/36, since there is a set of 36 possible combinations from repeated dice throws and 21 subsets in which the total is equal to 7 or more.

Joint probability is the compound occurrence of events so that the probability of the occurrence is $P(E,F) = P(E) P(F/E)$. Continuing the dice example, joint probability is stated thus: What is the probability of having one die A, of two dice, A and B, come up with a value equal to or greater than $4(E)$ and the total of the two dice to be equal to $7(F)$?

		Value of die #2 (F)					
		1	2	3	4	5	6
	1	2	3	4	5	6	7
	2	3	4	5	6	7	8
Value of die	3	4	5	6	7	8	9
#1 (E)	4	5	6	7	8	9	10
	5	6	7	8	9	10	11
	6	7	8	9	10	11	12

The diagram shows that there are three chances out of six to have the first die come up with a value of 4 or greater: $P(E) = 3/6$. The diagram also shows that given that the value of one die is 4 or more, then the probability of the total of two dice being 7 is $3/18$. The joint probability in this example is $(3/6)(3/18) = 1/12$.

Conditional probability is the chance occurrence of an event, given the probability of a state of nature, written as

$$P(E/F) = \frac{P(E \cap F)}{P(F)}$$

The equation is read as the probability of E, given the probability of F, is equal to the probability of the intersection of E and F (joint probability) divided by the probability of F. For the sake of an example, let us *assume* the following relationship between sex and education of the adult population:

	Male	Female	Total
	(F)		
Less than high school education	0.10	0.10	0.20
High school education	0.15	0.20	0.35
Some college education	0.15	0.10	0.25
College degree (E)	0.10	0.10	0.20
	0.50	0.50	1.00

What is the probability that a male adult (F) selected at random will have a college degree (E)? The complete probability distribution of the male adult education is

Education	Conditional Probability
Less than high school education	$\dfrac{0.10}{0.50} = 0.2$
High school education	$\dfrac{0.15}{0.50} = 0.3$
Some college education	$\dfrac{0.15}{0.50} = 0.3$
College degree	$\dfrac{0.10}{0.50} = 0.2$
Total	1.0

Shown in equation form,

$$P(E/F) = \frac{P(E \cap F)}{P(F)}$$

then the intersection of E and F is the probability of both a college degree education and a male shown as 0.10 in the data presentation. The probability of F (a male adult) is 0.50, also shown in the data example. The full equation is

$$P(E/F) = \frac{0.10}{0.50} \qquad \text{or } 0.2$$

which is the same conditional probability value shown in the probability distribution for male adults.

Posterior probability is a revision of prior probability on the basis of additional information. The statement for posterior probability is derived from the celebrated Bayes theorem[1]

$$P(A_i/E) = \frac{P(A_i)\,P(E/A_i)}{P(A_i)\,P(E/A_i) + \ldots + P(A_n)\,P(E/A_n)}$$

This theorem is applied to specific problems in the following sections of this chapter.

Usefulness of Computer Operations in Bayesian Analysis

The computer is useful in all three phases of Bayesian analysis: (1) determining prior probability, (2) determining posterior probability, and (3) determining various payoff alternatives. Business operations are sufficiently involved that a manager will benefit by having empirical data collected for computer computations. The manager still is in control of the analytical procedure, but would have the help of a computer for storage of data and analysis of data.

The computer is particularly useful in analysis of highly sophisticated Bayesian models involving many variables or many interrelationships, or both. In one example[2] management was interested in analyzing four alternative price levels for its product. Competition for the product included three other producers of a substitute product. The product was being distributed to four different market segments: A, B, C, and D. Market segments B, C, and D were functionally dependent on

---

[1] For an explanation see Halter, Albert N., and Dean, Gerald W. *Decisions Under Uncertainty*. Chicago: Southwestern Publishing, 1971 (pp. 26, 27).

[2] The case illustration is based on the example in Green, Paul E. Bayesian decision theory in pricing strategy. *Journal of Marketing* (January, 1963): 5–14.

segment *A*, so that sales increases in the latter market would result in follow-up sales in the other three. Prior probabilities for alternative states of nature under each alternative price level resulted in over 400 possible outcomes to be considered. Implementation of this Bayesian model was definitely aided by use of a computer. In addition, sensitivity testing could be accomplished through repeated computer runs merely by altering specific inputs in the model. Thus a decision maker can determine which factors in the analysis are most significant to the outcome.

APPLICATION OF BAYESIAN DECISION THEORY

Despite the lack of complete knowledge in a problem situation, the business manager is expected to make a decision. Bayesian decision theory has been developed in recent years to assist the business manager to arrive at more effective decisions in such a case. The Bayesian statistics approach includes a personalistic interpretation of probability. Decision makers can supply their own subjective estimate of a prior probability, that is, an estimate of chance occurrence of an action in an environment of uncertainty. Bases for prior probability range from the application of a sophisticated record of empirical observations to the use of intuition. Three examples of applying Bayesian analysis to business problems follow.

Competitive Bidding

A competitive bid may be offered at different levels: a high level relative to estimated costs, showing a large margin of profit, or at various lower levels with profit margins reduced accordingly. Obviously the high bid would have the most desirable projected profit, but the probabilities of success must also be considered, that is, the higher the bid, the lower the chances of winning the award. Bayesian decision theory provides a framework of analysis to indicate an optimum profit relationship between levels of bid and probable degree of success.

Before entering a bid competition, a decision maker should have some notion of probable success associated with different bid alternatives. His records of past bid experiences will provide a basis for prior probabilities and by applying the Bayesian analysis he can compute posterior probabilities, that is, estimates of states of nature, given additional knowledge about some event in the environment. For example, given a situation in which the Ace Company management must consider only one major competitor (C_1) in the bid competition, bidder C_1 will win the bid if the Ace Company bid is high; but if C_1 does not bid, the Ace Company will win the bid, even with a high bid. In a forthcoming bid competition the Ace Company executives estimated that a high bid yielding $200,000 profit would win if C_1 did not bid, but it would require a lower bid yielding only $50,000 profit to win the contract if C_1 did enter the competition. The profit table in this situation would be as follows:

Acts	S_1: Competitor 1 will bid	S_2: Competitor 1 will not bid
A_1: Bid high	0	$200,000
A_2: Bid low	$50,000	50,000

By examining past experience, Ace Company managers estimated that the prior probability that C_1 would enter the bidding for this contract was $P = 0.60$, leaving the prior probability that C_1 would not enter the bidding as $P = 0.40$. Payoff analysis of the information is

A_1: Bid high = (0.6) (0) + (0.4)($200,000) = $80,000
A_2: Bid low = (0.6) ($50,000) + (0.4)($50,000) = $50,000

Given the above prior probabilities, the optimum decision is to bid low (A_2).

Additional sophistication is provided to the analysis by computing posterior probabilities and applying them to the problem solution. Assume that the Ace Company executives had maintained records that indicate how often their estimate that C_1 would or would not bid was correct and that the result is as follows:

	Competitor 1 did bid	Competitor 1 did not bid
Expectation that C_1 would bid	0.70	0.40
Expectation that C_1 would not bid	0.30	0.60

Therefore C_1 had in fact entered the bidding 70 percent of the time that the Ace Company expected them to. However, 30 percent of the time C_1 entered the bidding unexpectedly. On the other hand, C_1 did not enter the bidding 60 percent of the time that the Ace Company did not expect them to. However, 40 percent of the time C_1 did not bid when the Ace Company expected them to.

Now posterior probabilities can be computed to modify the earlier payoff analysis, combining both the prior probabilities and the record of success in past estimates of prior probabilities. The results of the computation are given in Table 4-1.

TABLE 4-1

Computation of Posterior Probabilities

1 Success of Past Estimates of C_1's Actions	2	3	4	5	6
	Joint Probabilities		Marginal Probabilities	Posterior Probabilities	
	$P(S_1) \cdot P(R_i/S_1)$	$P(S_2) \cdot P(R_i/S_2)$	$P(R_i)$	$P(S_1/R_i)$	$P(S_2/R_i)$
R_1	0.42	0.16	0.58	0.724	0.276
R_2	0.18	0.24	0.42	0.429	0.571
$P(S_j)$	0.60	0.40	1.00		

For example, the probability that C_1 will enter the bidding (S_1) and that the Ace Company expectation that C_1 will enter the bidding is correct (R_1) is

$$P(S_1) \cdot P(R_1/S_1) = (0.60)(0.70) = 0.42$$

The other computations in columns 2 and 3 are conducted in the same fashion. Column 4 is the summation of the joint probabilities to become marginal probabilities. The posterior probabilities then answer the question: Given R_1, what is the probability that S_1 is true? For example, given R_1 (the record of successfully anticipating C_1 to bid 70 percent of the time), the probability of S_1 (that C_1 would enter a bid in the present circumstance) is

$$P(S_1/R_1) = \frac{0.42}{0.58} = 0.724$$

The modified payoff analysis of the competitive bid in the situation when the Ace Company has reason to expect C_1 to bid is now

A_1: Bid high $= (0.724)(0) + (0.276)(\$200,000) = \$55,200$
A_2: Bid low $= (0.875)(\$50,000) + (0.125)(\$50,000) = \$50,000$

Now evidence indicates a decision for the Ace Company management to bid high in order to optimize payoff with the application of posterior probabilities.

Application to Investment Portfolio Selection

Bayesian analysis is also useful in investment portfolio selection. A critical factor in the design of an investment portfolio is the economic outlook. Typically an investment manager makes implicit forecasts of the forthcoming economic environment before determining the investment portfolio holdings. He knows expected rate of return for various investment issues, such as savings and loan shares, government issues, blue-chip stock, and speculative stock, in both favorable and unfavorable economic circumstances. By considering implicit assumptions about the economic outlook and the ramifications on rates of return of various alternative investments, the investment manager proceeds to make his decision.

The application of Bayesian statistics, however, would improve the decision-making process by requiring that the decision maker assign explicit probabilities to the problem solution. In a simple illustration,[3] assume the following:

Acts	S_1: Rate of return in prosperity (percent)	S_2: Rate of return in recession (percent)
A_1: Aggressive investments	8	2
A_2: Conservative investments	5	4

Given that the current year is a prosperous one, the investor has prior knowledge that prosperous years are followed by recession years 40 percent of the time. Payoff analysis of the investment opportunities is

A_1: Aggressive investments $= (0.60)(8\%) + (0.4)(2\%) = 5.6\%$

A_2: Conservative investments $= (0.60)(5\%) + (0.4)(4\%) = 4.6\%$

---

[3] For a more sophisticated example see Mao, James C. T., and Sarndal, Carl E. A decision theory approach to portfolio selection. *Management Science*, 12(April, 1966): B323–B333.

Applying Bayesian analysis, posterior probabilities are computed based on additional information. In this case the investor learns that a leading forecaster has predicted that the approaching year will be a prosperous one. The forecaster's record of accuracy is as follows:

	S_1: Prosperous year	S_2: Recession year
R_1: Prediction of a prosperous year	0.85	0.10
R_2: Prediction of a recession year	0.15	0.90

On balance, the forecaster had a high degree of success in his predictions: He was correct when he predicted future prosperity 85 percent of the time.

Computation of the posterior probabilities, incorporating the additional forecast information with the prior probabilities, is shown in Table 4–2. Consequently, knowing that the prior probability for a prosperous year to be followed by another prosperous year is 0.60 and that a leading forecaster with a known record of success has predicted another prosperous year, the investor now has a posterior probability of 0.927 for anticipating a favorable economic outlook. The revised payoff table is

A_1: Aggressive investments $= (0.927)(8\%) + (0.073)(2\%) = 7.56\%$
A_2: Conservative investments $= (0.20)(5\%) + (0.80)(4\%) = 4.2\%$

Obviously, on the basis of the Bayesian analysis the investor would be maximizing his payoff by investing aggressively at this time.

TABLE 4–2

1	2	3	4	5	6
Fore-caster's Predic-tions	Joint Probabilities		Marginal Probabilities	Posterior Probabilities	
	$P(S_1) \cdot P(R_i/S_1)$	$P(S_2) \cdot P(R_i/S_2)$	$P(R_i)$	$P(S_1/R_i)$	$P(S_2/R_i)$
R_1	0.51	0.04	0.55	0.927	0.073
R_2	0.09	0.36	0.45	0.20	0.80
$P(S_j)$	0.60	0.40	1.00		

Product Development Decisions

Bayesian decision theory is helpful for measuring the cost–benefits of conducting market tests designed to determine the likelihood of success in introducing new products. Exploratory research or past experience can provide a basis for determining prior probabilities of varying degrees of success for new product sales—for example, 0.65 that the new product sales will be 15 percent of the market (S_1), 0.25 that 5 percent of the market will be captured (S_2), and 0.10 that only 1 percent of the market will be captured (S_3). A payoff analysis A can be computed by multiplying profits related to the three different levels of market share success and the respective prior probabilities.

At this point Bayesian decision theory can be introduced to determine a cost–benefit analysis of conducting further marketing research, which would modify the prior probability values into posterior probability values.[4] Success of previous management estimates of market share based on marketing research studies can be determined; for example, when company marketing research data in the past have indicated that 10 percent of the market would be captured by a new product (R_1), experience showed that the company did accomplish this feat 70 percent of the time. Joint probabilities of $P(S_1) \cdot P(R_i/S_1)$ and $P(S_2) \cdot P(R_i/S_2)$ can be computed to establish a basis for developing posterior probabilities. Following computations of posterior probabilities, a new payoff analysis B is computed by multiplying posterior probabilities and profit amounts at the various states of nature. The difference between payoff analysis A and payoff analysis B is the benefit of additional marketing research. Comparing this dollar benefit against cost of the marketing research, a decision maker would obviously conduct further research if the benefits exceeded the cost but not if the cost exceeded the expected benefits.

SUMMARY

Bayesian decision theory affords a decision maker an additional framework of analysis, along with classical statistical analysis, to make effective decisions operating in an environment of uncertainty, which is the typical business situation. The business manager is able to apply subjective probability values to alternative states of nature. These subjective estimates begin as prior probabilities, but are modified into posterior probabilities with the addition of knowledge about some event in the problem. Application of the posterior probabilities in a payoff analysis provides a basis for optimizing problem solution.

---

[4] For an illustrative problem solution see Pessemier, Edgar A. *New Product Decisions.* New York: McGraw-Hill, 1966 (pp. 119–130).

CHAPTER 5

Linear Programming Model

The concept of linear programming dates back many years in the history of mathematical theory. It was not until 1947, however, that formalization of the concept with a specific area of interest and a name was originated by George B. Dantzig, a mathematician for the United States Air Force.[1] Much has been written about linear programming in textbooks and articles since that time. There had been limited applications of the technique to business problems until the widespread availability of the computer because of the computational difficulties involved. Now it is possible to obtain a rapid solution to highly complex problems by plugging appropriate data into a "canned" computer program and running it through a computer. More will be said about such programs at the end of this chapter. It is necessary to understand the computational procedure in order to interpret computer results. The goal is not only achievement of an optimal solution, but also awareness of what changes can be made in the business operations and the subsequent effect on profits.

CONCEPT OF LINEAR PROGRAMMING

Linear programming is a technique for allocating scarce resources among competing alternatives according to some criterion to be optimized (maximum profits, minimum costs, least time). The model includes a linear objective function (maximization criterion expressed in mathematical form), constraints of the problem, and choice variables. A solution is a set of values for the choice variables, values that satisfy all of the constraints. The optimum solution is one for which the objective

---

[1] Springer, C., Herlihy, R., and Beggs, R. *Advanced Methods and Models*. Homewood, Ill.: Richard D. Irwin, 1965 (p. 202).

function value is at an optimum. The linear programming model is designed to produce an optimum solution from among nonnegative alternatives.

Problems in business lend themselves to this concept since the factors of production in business are scarce resources which must be allocated among different possible uses. There are specific requirements in the problem situation that must exist before a linear programming model should be applied:[2]

1. Management has selected an objective function that will measure the optimality of any proposed solution. There is a choice among alternatives to achieve a desired goal.
2. There are scarce resources and these restraints must be known.
3. The objective function and the restraints can be expressed algebraically.
4. The objective function and the restraints in the problem situation must be linear.

There are several approaches to the solution of linear programming models such as graphic solution, algebraic solution, and simplex solution. The graphic solution is useful in elementary problems containing two or three variables. Two variables can be drawn in graphic form in a two-dimensional mode and an optimum solution computed. Three variables can be shown in a three-dimensional graphic form, but there is a likelihood that accuracy is reduced, limiting the practical use of the graphic method to problems with two variables. Although the algebraic solution can handle more than three variables, it is not an efficient method. The simplex method is the easiest and quickest approach to finding an optimum solution. A detailed description of the graphic solution is presented in the next section, followed by an explanation of the algebraic method and a conceptual presentation of the simplex method.

The Graphic Solution

The graphic solution is a procedure of plotting the problem elements on graph paper. The problem variables are plotted along coordinates, so that given two variables, one will be shown as the X coordinate and the other variable will be shown as the Y coordinate. The restraining elements are plotted as linear relationships according to given

---

[2] Naylor, T., Byrne, E., and Vernon, J. *Introduction to Linear Programming.* Belmont, Calif.: Wadsworth, 1971 (pp. 9, 10).

equations. If there is a solution to the problem, the lines on the graph will enscribe a multisided figure known as a *feasible set*, which contains a number of possible solution points all of which satisfy the problem constraint. (It is conceivable that no feasible set will result from the graphing, in which case there is no solution to the linear programming problem.)

An example of the graphic solution up to this point is as follows: A bicycle manufacturer can produce two different bicycles, one for adults (B_a) and one for children (B_c). Each of these bicycles requires three different manufacturing steps: forming, assembly, and painting. The requirements in hours for each step per unit for the bicycles are

	$\underline{B_a}$	$\underline{B_c}$
Forming	2	4
Assembly	6	3
Painting	3	1

The available capacities of these steps in hours for a given time period are (1) forming, 200; (2) assembly, 300; and (3) painting, 120. The profit is $20 for each unit of B_a and $10 for each unit of B_c; thus the objective function is

$$P = 20B_a + 10B_c$$

The variables B_a and B_c must be nonnegative. It is assumed that the firm can sell all that it manufactures.

The first step in the graphic solution is to label two coordinates B_a and B_c and proceed to diagram different values for the objective function. If a value of $800 is assumed for P, then the objective function is

$$\$800 = 20B_a + 10B_c$$

A line can be drawn to represent this function as shown in Figure 5–1 by locating two points: B_a is 40 when B_c is 0 and B_c is 80 when B_a is 0. Assuming a value of $1000, the objective function is

$$\$1200 = 20B_a + 10B_c$$

and the extreme points are B_a is 60 when B_c is 0 and B_c is 120 when B_a is 0. This line is also shown in Figure 5–1. Other lines can be shown for other values selected for the objective function. These lines would parallel the two that have been graphed in Figure 5–1.

The next step in the graphic solution is to diagram the problem constraints. The first constraint given is in the forming operation. It takes 2 hours to form the parts for B_a and 4 hours to form the parts of B_c,

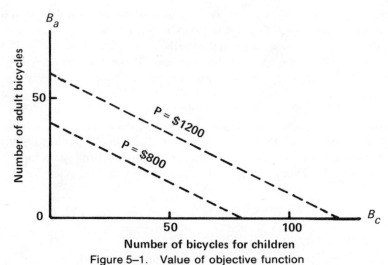

Figure 5–1. Value of objective function

with a total capacity of 200 hours for forming. Therefore the linear equation is

$$2B_a + 4B_c \leq 200$$

The relevant area is shown beneath the shaded line AB in Figure 5–2. When the number of children's bikes B_c is kept to zero, the 100 adult bikes shown at point A can be formed. But when the number of adult bikes B_a is kept at zero, the 50 children's bikes can be formed. Various combinations of the two types of bikes can be formed between these two extremes.

The second constraint given is in the assembly operation. It takes 6 hours to assemble B_a and 3 hours to assemble B_c, with a total capacity of 300 hours for assembly. Therefore the linear equation is

$$6B_a + 3B_c \leq 300$$

The addition of this constraint CD is shown in Figure 5–3. The extreme points are B_a is 50 at point C when B_c is 0 and B_c is 100 at point D when B_a is 0.

The final constraint given is the painting operation. It takes 3 hours to paint B_a and 1 hour to paint B_c, with a total capacity of 120 hours for painting. Therefore the linear equation is

$$3B_a + 1B_c \leq 120$$

The graph with all three constraints is shown in Figure 5–4. The extreme

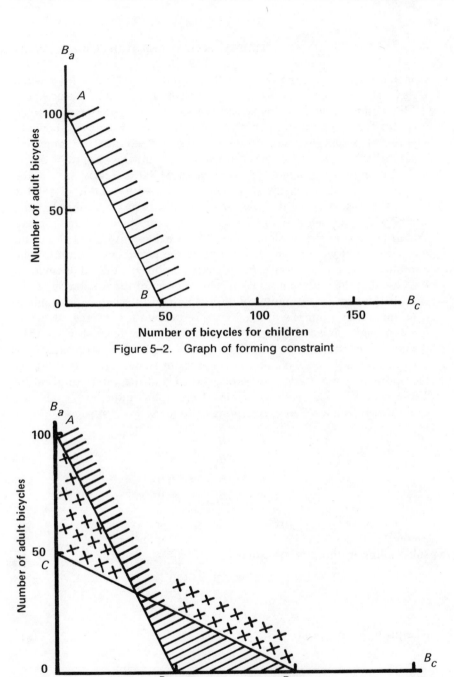

Figure 5–2. Graph of forming constraint

Figure 5–3. Graph of assembly constraint

points are B_a is 40 at point E when B_c is 0 and B_c is 120 at point F when B_a is 0. The feasible set of solution points is thus described as the figure $0EPB$. Points outside of this set do not satisfy all of the restraints. To solve for the optimum solution, the diagram of the feasible set shown in Figure 5–4 is superimposed upon the lines that represent the objective function in Figure 5–1 resulting in the graph shown as Figure 5–5.

The objective function with a value of $1200 is clearly outside the feasibility set. Although the objective function with a value of $800 is within the feasibility set, it is clear that it can be increased somewhat and still be within the set. A parallel shift of the linear objective function can extend upward in the feasible set until it coincides with point P, but no further, since it would then violate one of the problem constraints. The optimum solution is point P, a confirmation of the mathematical theorem that the optimum solution is at a corner of the feasible set. (It is conceivable that an optimum solution may have alternative possibilities —in the given example if the linear representation of the objective function had coincided with a boundary line of the feasibility set, then the corners connecting the boundary line would have equal profitability and the manager could choose on the basis of some other criterion). At the optimum point P, the value for B_a is 28 and the value for B_c is 36. These values could be read from the graphic indicators and also computed by simultaneous equations as follows:

$$2B_a + 4B_c = 200$$
$$3B_a + 1B_c = 120$$

$$
\begin{array}{rcl}
2B_a + 4B_c &=& 200 \\
12B_a + 4B_c &=& 480 \\
\hline
-10B_a &=& -280 \\
B_a &=& 28
\end{array}
$$

substituting in the original equation

$$3(28) + 1B_c = 120$$
$$1B_c = 120 - 84$$
$$B_c = 36$$

The profit at this point is

$$\$20(28) + \$10(36) = \$920$$

The optimum solution would be to produce 28 adult bicycles and 36 bicycles for children.

The shortcoming of the graphic method is obvious when the number of variables in the problem increases. As stated earlier, the graphic

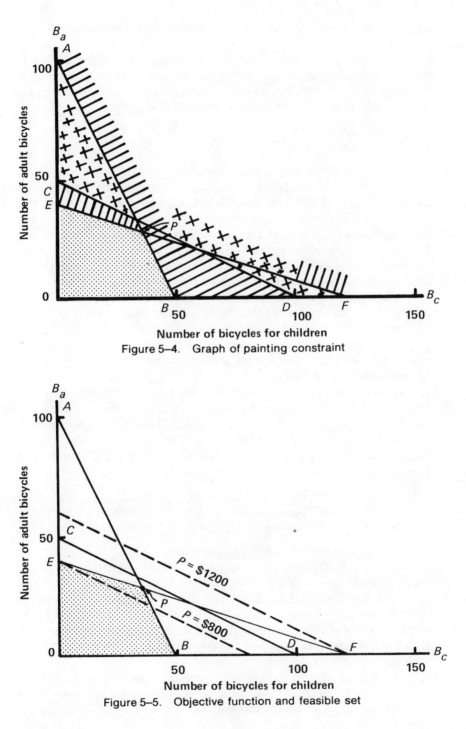

Figure 5–4.   Graph of painting constraint

Figure 5–5.   Objective function and feasible set

method is practical for solving only linear programming problems with two variables. Beyond that number, the simplex method of solution is recommended. An explanation of the algebraic method is presented next as a prelude to an understanding of the simplex method.

The Algebraic Method

The algebraic method is a mathematical approach to solving linear programming problems. It is not limited to the number of variables that can be included in the problem situation as is the graphic method. The utilization of the algebraic method, however, is a cumbersome and inefficient procedure as will be observed in the following explanation. The reason for including the explanation is to establish a basic understanding of procedure leading to the simplex method, which is the recommended approach to solving linear programming problems.

It was pointed out earlier that the optimum solution is located at one of the corners of the feasible set in a linear programming problem. The methodology in the algebraic method is an analysis of the individual corners in the feasible set, beginning with the point of origin, and proceeding with an analysis of each consecutive corner until the optimum point is located.

The first step in the algebraic method is to convert the restricting inequations of the problem into equations by adding what are known as "slack variables." The slack variables are designated by letters such as d, e, and f; one for each inequation. Using data from the bicycle manufacturing example shown in the preceding section, the conversion is as follows:

$$2B_a + 4B_c \leq 200 \quad \text{becomes} \quad 2B_a + 4B_c + d = 200 \tag{1.1}$$
$$6B_a + 3B_c \leq 300 \quad \text{becomes} \quad 6B_a + 3B_c + e = 300 \tag{2.1}$$
$$3B_a + 1B_c \leq 120 \quad \text{becomes} \quad 3B_a + 1B_c + f = 120 \tag{3.1}$$

The slack variable must be nonnegative.

As shown in Figure 5–6, the value of the slack constraints along the linear constraints is equal to zero, and the value of B_a and B_c is zero along the coordinates. Each corner of the set will have two variables equal to zero plus a unique value for each of the other variables in the problem, which in this example is three. The variables with unique values are known as basic variables and the two variables that are equal to zero are known as zero variables.

The second step in the algebraic method is to analyze one of the corners of the feasible set for optimality; the easiest one to begin with is the point of origin where B_a is zero and B_c is zero. The equations are

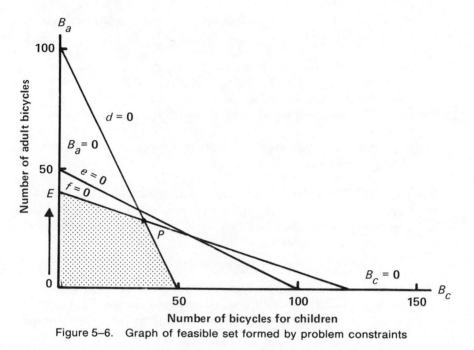

Figure 5–6. Graph of feasible set formed by problem constraints

written with the zero variable on the right side and the basic variables on the left side. The group of equations at the point of origin is

Objective function: $P = 20B_a + 10B_c$

$$d = 200 - 2B_a - 4B_c \qquad (1.2)$$

$$e = 300 - 6B_a - 3B_c \qquad (2.2)$$

$$f = 120 - 3B_a - 1B_c \qquad (3.2)$$

The corner at the point of origin is determined not to be optimum because at least one of the zero variables in the objective function has a positive coefficient. Any change in the zero variable to a positive value will increase the objective function, so a shift is made to analyze another corner of the feasible set for optimality.

The shift procedure is a change in value of the zero variable (B_a or B_c) that has the largest positive coefficient. The change should be the maximum amount possible within the problem constraints. When this change is completed, another variable will become a zero variable at another corner of the analysis. In the example, B_a has a larger positive coefficient than B_c and will be changed. The limits to the change are shown by the following:

(1.2) B_a can be increased to 100 within the constraint of $d = 200 - 2B_a - 4B_c$ (B_c is a zero variable). Beyond $B_a = 100$, the slack variable would become negative.

(1.3) B_a can be increased to 50 within the constraint of $e = 300 - 6B_a - 3B_c$.

(1.4) B_a can be increased to 40 within the constraint of $f = 120 - 3B_a - 1B_c$.

The most that B_a can be increased within the problem constraints then is 40. The next corner to analyze in the feasible set by the shift procedure has values of $B_a = 40$ and $f = 0$ (shown as point E in Figure 5–6).

The limiting equation

$$f = 120 - 3B_a - 1B_c$$

is changed to obtain the new set of equations so that the new basic variable B_a is placed to the left and the new zero variable f is placed to the right. Transposition of the equation results in the new equation

$$B_a = \frac{120 - 1B_c - f}{3}$$

The new value for B_a is substituted in the objective function and the group of constraining equations. The objective function becomes

$$P = 20\left(\frac{120 - 1B_c - f}{3}\right) + 10B_c$$

or

$$P = 800 + \frac{10B_c}{3} - \frac{20f}{3}$$

The new group of equations is

$$d = 200 - 2\left(\frac{120 - 1B_c - f}{3}\right) - 4B_c = 120 - \frac{10B_c}{3} + \frac{2f}{3} \qquad (1.3)$$

$$e = 300 - 6\left(\frac{120 - 1B_c - f}{3}\right) - 3B_c = 60 - 1B_c + 2f \qquad (2.3)$$

$$B_a = \frac{120 - 1B_c - f}{3} \qquad (3.3)$$

Again the analysis shows that at least one of the zero variables in the objective function has a positive coefficient, therefore this corner is not the optimal solution.

The next step is to shift the analysis once again to another corner of the feasible set in the same manner as above. The zero variable B_c in the new objective function has the larger positive coefficient and is increased in value to the maximum amount possible within the problem constraints. An examination of the equations indicates that the value of B_c could be changed to 36 in equation (1.3), to 60 in equation (2.3), and to 120 in equation (3.3). Therefore the most that B_c can be increased before violating one of the constraints is 36 and the new limiting equation has the slack variable d. (The shift as shown in Figure 5–6 is from point E to point P.) The limiting equation is changed so that the new basic variable B_c is placed to the left and the new zero variable d is placed to the right,

$$B_c = 36 + \frac{f}{5} - \frac{3d}{10}$$

Substituting the new value for B_c in the objective function will indicate whether the new corner is the optimal solution; if not, the whole procedure of shifting to another corner is repeated. The graph of new equations in the bicycle example is

Objective function:

$$P = 800 + \frac{10}{3}\left(36 + \frac{f}{5} - \frac{3d}{10}\right) - \frac{20f}{3} = 920 - 6f - d$$

$$B_c = 36 + \frac{f}{5} - \frac{3d}{10} \tag{1.4}$$

$$e = 60 - \left(36 + \frac{f}{5} - \frac{3d}{10}\right) + 2f = 24 + \frac{9f}{5} + \frac{3d}{10} \tag{2.4}$$

$$B_a = 40 - \frac{1}{3}\left(36 + \frac{f}{5} - \frac{3d}{10}\right) - \frac{f}{3} = 28 - \frac{2f}{5} + \frac{d}{10} \tag{3.4}$$

The value for the objective function of 920 at this corner is optimal since the coefficient of each zero variable is negative. The value of B_c at this optimum point, as indicated in equation (1.4), is 36 and the value of B_a, as indicated in equation (3.4), is 28. These values are the same answers as determined by the graphic solution represented by point P in Figure 5–6. Although the algebraic method is superior to the graphic method, it is a cumbersome and inefficient method to use in problems that contain the relatively large number of constraint equations found in most business problems. The recommended solution procedure is the simplex method presented next.

The Simplex Method

The simplex method is an efficient means for solving linear programming problems that have more than three variables. The solution procedure follows the iterative process described in the algebraic method. The procedure represents tedious calculations in the solution process when attempted by manual means. The solution fortunately, however, follows an iterative process that is ideally suited for computer operations and for which various prepared solution programs are readily available. The General Electric Company, for example, had developed such a program in the early 1960s identified as CD225D7.005, which could handle problems having as many as 300 constraint equations and the number of choice variables limited only by tape capacity.[3] A manager need merely state the objective function and the restrictions in a form acceptable to the computer and the computations are performed by the machine. Other linear programming packages are available from computer manufacturers.

An understanding of the simplex solution is desirable if a manager is to interpret computer printouts in an effective manner. As a first step in the programmed solution, the computer is instructed to check for an existing feasible set. It is possible that no such set exists in the problem, meaning that the problem as formulated does not have a solution. The manager must then review the make-up of the problem for possible revision in order to obtain a basis for a solution.

If the computer determines that a feasible set does exist, it continues to operate according to instructions similar to the algebraic method until an optimum solution is discovered. The total procedure is summarized as follows:

1. The problem should be identified in terms of a linear objective function.
2. Slack variables should be added to convert inequalities into equalities.
3. A simplex table should be developed for a basic feasible solution.
4. Variables should be identified as basic or nonbasic if the solution is not optimum.
5. A new simplex table incorporating the changes in step (4) should be developed.
6. The actions in steps (4) and (5) should be repeated until an optimum solution is achieved.

In the simplex solution of the bicycle manufacturing example, data were keypunched on five separate computer cards to supply the

---

[3] Springer, *op. cit.*, p. 233.

computer with the necessary problem information about constraints, variables, and the objective function. These five cards were added to a "canned" computer program designed to solve linear programming problems. The computer printout is shown in Exhibit 5–1. The answers are identical to those received by the other solution methods: Optimum solution is to produce 28 adult bicycles and 36 bicycles for children with a profit of $920 as the objective function.

```
PROBLEM NUMBER                   1

2              VARIABLES
3              CONSTRAINTS
OBJECTIVE IS TO BE MAXIMIZED

CONSTRAINT     VARIABLE        VALUE

1              1               2
1              2               4
1              MAXIMUM         200
2              1               6
2              2               3
2              MAXIMUM         300
3              1               3
3              2               1
3              MAXIMUM         120
OBJECTIVE      1               20
OBJECTIVE      2               10
FEASIBLE SOLUTION FOUND AFTER                  2              ITERATIONS
ITERATION      3               OBJECTIVE =
ITERATION      4               OBJECTIVE =
ITERATION      5               OBJECTIVE =
VARIABLES IN THE SOLUTION
  VARIABLE     2               AMOUNT =        36
  VARIABLE     1               AMOUNT =        28

VARIABLES OUT OF THE SOLUTION

BINDING CONSTRAINTS
  CONSTRAINT   3               SHADOW PRICE = 6.
  CONSTRAINT   1               SHADOW PRICE = 1

SLACK CONSTRAINTS
  CONSTRAINT   2               SLACK =         24

OBJECTIVE IS   920
```

Exhibit 5–1. Computer printout of linear programming solution

Sensitivity analysis. The foregoing solution is based on fixed existing amounts of resources. Sensitivity analysis is a study of potential profit impact from increases in the given resources similar to marginal analysis. The objective is to determine if an increase in one of the resources would increase the solution payoff.

The potential payoff can be shown graphically if the problem contains only two variables. Returning to the bicycle manufacturing example in Figure 5–7, we again show the forming operation as AB, the assembly operation as CD, the painting resource as EF, the optimum point as P, and the objective function as the dashed line. The graph shows that the assembly operation CD is not a binding constraint on the solution. Rather, it is the forming operation AB that is the binding constraint. The feasibility set would expand as AB is shifted to A^1B^1 at point Q. It is not profitable to increase the forming operations beyond point Q because the assembly operation becomes binding at that point. Therefore point Q is a new optimum point as a result of increasing resources for the forming operation. There would be a new profit solution represented by the linear objective function drawn through point Q. (A similar analysis could be performed by adding resources to the painting operation EF and shifting the optimum point to R.) A manager could compare the marginal cost of adding additional resources into one of the operations with the marginal revenue from increased sales of the additional production.

The potential profit for each additional feasible unit is called the "shadow price." This shadow price can be computed mathematically.[4] The computer program for solving linear programming problems has the beneficial feature in that it will indicate shadow prices for the different variables in the solution printout. In Exhibit 5–1 the computer printout shows constraint 3, painting operation, with a shadow price of $6.00 whereas constraint 1, forming operation, has a shadow price of $1. This means that it would be more profitable to increase the resources in the painting operation, resulting in a net profit of $6 for each additional *feasible* unit produced until the level of the new optimum point is reached. The new optimum point is determined by the amount of slack in other constraints, which in this example is 24 hours of unused capacity in constraint 2, assembly operation. Additional resources to the painting operation beyond point Q would not be profitable because the assembly operation would be a binding constraint, being used to full capacity at point Q.

Application of Linear Programming to Capital Budgeting[5]

Use of linear programming in capital budgeting can provide a greater sophistication to the analysis, which in turn can result in greater profits. Traditional capital budgeting compares the cost savings that result from the purchase of new equipment to the cost of the new equipment. In an example of a manufacturer who is considering the

---

[4] For example, see Brabb, George J. *Introduction to Quantitative Management.* New York: Holt, Rinehart and Winston, 1968 (pp. 83–85).

[5] This example is based on the article by Garrison, Ray H. Linear programming in capital budgeting. *Management Accounting*, 52(April, 1971): 43–46.

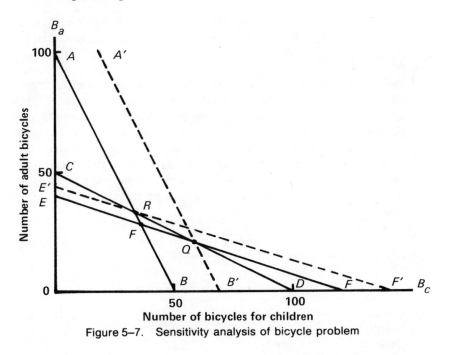

Figure 5–7. Sensitivity analysis of bicycle problem

purchase of three new shaping machines, the traditional analysis shows the cost savings possible with the addition of the three new machines (Table 5–1).

TABLE 5–1

Product	Units Produced per Month	Per Unit Cost Savings	Total Cost Savings per Month
Surf boards	1120	$1.36	$1523.20
Tow boards	850	0.34	289.00
Flying saucers	180	1.02	183.60
	2150		$1995.80

Assuming the company desires a 20-percent time-adjusted rate of return on all investments, the present value of the cost savings over the 8-year life of the machines is $91,895 ($1995.80 × 12 months = $23,949.60 plus 20 percent gain for 8 years which is

$67,945.40). The cost of the three new machines, at $35,000 each, is a total of $105,000. The decision based on the above analysis would be to reject the purchase proposal since the cost exceeds the anticipated payoff.

The application of linear programming adds another element to the analysis. Instead of accepting the product mix as a constant, the manager can simulate the addition of the new shaping machines in the manufacturing process to alter the product mix according to a maximization of product contribution to profit. The assumption is that the company can sell all that it produces. Utilization of the linear programming technique to the expanded capital equipment showed a change in optimal product mix and increased profit (Table 5–2).

TABLE 5–2

Product	Change in Units Produced	Unit Contribution Margin	Net Change
Surf boards	680	$11.36	$7724.80
Tow boards	(500)	9.34	(4670.00)
Flying saucers	(180)	9.02	(1623.60)
	0		$1431.20

The result shows an increase in the production of surf boards of 680, a reduction of tow boards of 500, and an elimination of flying saucers since 180 were all that had been originally produced. Since more units of surf boards, which contributes the highest profit per unit, are included in the revised product mix total, there is an increase in total profit due to the change in types of types produced. The increased profit is shown to be $1431.20 per month or $17,1740.40. The addition of this amount to the annual cost savings due to the new equipment of $23,949.60 gives a total of $41,124.00. The present value of $41,124 at 20 percent for 8 years is $157,793. The purchase proposal becomes feasible since the cost of the three new machines is $105,000.

Application of Linear Programming to Media Allocation

Analysis of the media allocation problem can benefit from the use of linear programming. This problem has the characteristics required by the linear programming technique.

1. Management has an objective function, usually stated in terms of maximizing advertising exposures to a designated audience.
2. There are scarce resources in terms of budget and media availability.
3. The problem elements can be expressed algebraically.
4. The elements in the problem can be assumed to be linear although it should be recognized that successive purchases of a given medium may have diminishing returns.

In one reference[6] there is an example of a media allocation problem to spend $1,000,000 on advertising women's electric razors in consumer magazines using full-page, four-color, nonbleed advertisements. Twelve magazines judged appropriate to reach the desired audience were selected. Each of these magazines was classified by an effectiveness rating procedure (readership characteristics of the magazine relevant to the purchase potential for women's electric razors plus size of circulation of the magazine divided by the advertising rate of the magazine) so as to determine an "effective readings per dollar spent" index. The objective function for the problem became a maximization of the summation of the above index for each of the 12 magazines:

$$\text{maximum function} = 158X_1 + 263X_2 + 106X_3 + 108X_4 + 65X_5 + 176X_6 + 285X_7 + 86X_8 + 120X_9 + 51X_{10} + 190X_{11} + 101X_{12}$$

The budgetary constraint was

$$X_1 + X_2 + \cdots + X_{12} \leq 1{,}000{,}000$$

Aside from the usual nonnegativity constraint, the analyst can place other specific constraints to the format of the problem. One possibility is to limit the dollar allocation for a monthly magazine to the cost of 12 ads per year, eliminating the possible occurrence of more than one ad in the same issue. The total problem is then run through a computer to obtain the optimum allocation of the budget among the 12 magazines.

The above example restricted the media allocation alternatives only to magazines. Another approach would be to include all types of media as alternatives. The new problem situation would not be as clean cut, however. There is the complication of standardizing different media; radio, television, newspaper, magazine, on the basis of cost. One possible means of standardization is a similar procedure to that in the above example to determine an "effective readings per dollar spent" index. Then the objective function would be to maximize the summation of the indices of the various media. The solution is thus designed to indicate the optimum dollar allocation among all available media.

---

[6] Engel, James F., and Warshaw, Martin R. Allocating advertising dollars by linear programming. *Journal of Advertising Research*, 4(September, 1964): 42–48.

CONCLUSION

The linear programming technique is a very useful tool in determining maximum profit or least-cost solutions to many resource allocation problems. A primary prerequisite to use of this technique is a linear relationship in the costs and revenue factors, a situation that can be found in business operations. Once a manager has designed a problem format, the computations are easily accomplished by utilization of prepared computer programs. Sensitivity analysis and shadow prices are included in the computer printout, providing a manager with guidelines for improved decision making.

CHAPTER 6

Queuing Theory

Queuing problems known as "waiting-line" problems are common situations in the business world. Such problems have beginnings in production operations in which an operator not only waits for a machine to complete a job, but also waits for goods in process to reach his station. The other end of the business spectrum involves the distribution of finished goods or services to a waiting line of ultimate consumers. Queuing theory is a quantitative study of waiting lines. The probable length of the waiting line and the average time required in waiting can be compared to the cost of providing resources to alter the waiting-line situation. A decision maker would have a basis for optimizing the cost–benefit relationship in the waiting-line situation—supplying a sufficient amount of resources to produce a maximum result within minimum cost requirements.

The different elements of a queuing model are as follows:

1. Arrival: An input that appears at a facility for service.
2. Arrival rate: The average number of arrivals per unit of time.
3. Service time: The length of time required to service an incoming unit.
4. Service rate: The average number of units processed per unit of time.
5. Probabilities of specific occurrences caused by the waiting line.

These elements of a queuing model can appear in different relationships:

1. One line: One server

$$\text{INPUT} \quad \text{XXXX} \quad \longrightarrow \quad \text{OUTPUT}$$
$$0$$
one server

2. One line: Multiple servers

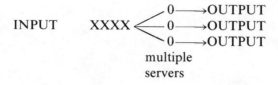

3. Multiple-line: Multiple servers (with and without line switching):

$$
\text{INPUT}\quad
\left.
\begin{array}{l}
\text{XXXX} \\
\text{XXXX} \\
\text{XXXX}
\end{array}
\right\}
\quad
\begin{array}{l}
0 \longrightarrow \text{OUTPUT} \\
0 \longrightarrow \text{OUTPUT} \\
0 \longrightarrow \text{OUTPUT}
\end{array}
$$

4. Single station to station:

INPUT   XXXX $_0 \longrightarrow$ XXXX $_0 \longrightarrow$ XXXX $_0 \longrightarrow$ OUTPUT

5. Multiple station to station (with and without line switching):

$$
\text{INPUT}
\left.
\begin{array}{l}
\text{XXXX} \\
\text{XXXX} \\
\text{XXXX}
\end{array}
\right\}
\begin{array}{l}
0 \longrightarrow \text{XXXX} \\
0 \longrightarrow \text{XXXX} \\
0 \longrightarrow \text{XXXX}
\end{array}
\left.
\begin{array}{l}
\\
\\
\end{array}
\right\}
\begin{array}{l}
0 \longrightarrow \text{XXXX} \\
0 \longrightarrow \text{XXXX} \\
0 \longrightarrow \text{XXXX}
\end{array}
\begin{array}{l}
0 \longrightarrow \text{OUTPUT} \\
0 \longrightarrow \text{OUTPUT} \\
0 \longrightarrow \text{OUTPUT}
\end{array}
$$

Mathematicians have developed equations to solve queuing problems in each of the different relationships. The actual computations were cumbersome until the advent of computers, which have enabled analysts to arrive at solutions quickly and without effort.

MATHEMATICAL FOUNDATION OF QUEUING THEORY

There are two approaches to solving queuing problems: the statistical approach and the simulation approach. The statistical approach requires that the input follow a pattern in which there is a small probability of occurrence in a given time, such as the number of customers arriving at a checkout station during a very short period of time. The technical term to describe this pattern is "Poisson distribution," named after the French statistician, Denis Poisson, who is one of the forefathers of modern statistics. When a Poisson distribution situation exists, an analyst can utilize standard equations in computing his results. An example of this approach is shown later in this chapter in determining the number of checkout stations in a supermarket.

The underlying assumptions in the statistical approach for solving queuing problems are as follows:

1. The probability of the occurrence of a success or failure is constant.
2. The probability of a success or failure is independent of what has previously happened.
3. The probability of an occurrence or a change during a time interval is approximately proportional to that time interval provided that it is small.
4. The probability of more than one occurrence or change during any small time interval is approximately zero when compared to the probability of a single change during that interval.[1]

The procedure for utilizing the statistical approach is to gather empirical data, which become the basis for computations. Guidelines suggested by Panico[2] for collecting data are (1) to make certain that data gathered are representative and do not constitute a specialized case; (2) to list the data used in solving the problem; (3) to express the mean arrival rate and the mean service rate in equivalent terms such as hours; (4) to determine whether input data comes from a finite or infinite population.

Different mathematical formulas have been derived for different types of queuing relationships.[3] The example to be presented is the most fundamental situation of one line and one server (infinite population). The relative mathematical formulas are (a is number of arrival and s is service time) as follows:

1. Expected number being serviced plus waiting:

$$E_n = \frac{a}{s - a}$$

2. Expected number in the waiting line:

$$E_w = \frac{a^2}{s(s - a)}$$

3. Expected waiting time in line:

$$E_t = \frac{E_w}{a} = \frac{a}{s(s - a)}$$

4. Expected waiting time in system:

$$E_s = E_t + \frac{1}{s} = \frac{1}{s - a}$$

---

[1] Panico, Joseph A. *Queuing Theory*. Englewood Cliffs, N.J.: Prentice-Hall, 1969 (p. 73).
[2] *Ibid.*, p. 53.
[3] For a complete presentation, see Panico's text, above, pp. 53–67.

(Restriction: First come–first served discipline.)

Assume that an empirical study of a supermarket with one checkout station revealed that an average of 20 people arrived per hour and that the clerk could check out 30 people per hour. Solutions to the above mathematical formulas would be as follows:

1. The expected number being serviced plus waiting is

$$E_n = \frac{a}{s - a} = \frac{20}{(30 - 20)} = \frac{20}{10} = 2 \text{ persons}$$

2. The expected number in the waiting line is

$$E_w = \frac{a^2}{s(s - a)} = \frac{20^2}{30(30 - 20)} = \frac{400}{300} = 1\frac{1}{3} \text{ persons}$$

3. The expected waiting time in line is

$$E_t = \frac{E_w}{a} = \frac{1\frac{1}{3}}{20} = \frac{4}{60} \text{ hour}$$

4. The expected waiting time in the system is

$$E_s = E_t + \frac{1}{s} = \frac{4}{60} + \frac{1}{30} = \frac{6}{60} \text{ hour}$$

The solution in the supermarket example characterizes the waiting-line situation to the manager. He could examine the results against the expectation of customers. If he increased the number of checkout stations, he would reduce the waiting time involved and provide better service, but his costs would increase. What he would have to determine is the effect of alternative actions on sales and profits. The key economic consideration is would improving service increase sales and profits sufficiently to more than cover the costs of expansion?

EMPIRICAL EXAMPLE

A more complex example utilizing actual empirical data of the quantity of boats and barges processed monthly by an Ohio River dam involving one line–one service (infinite population) is given by Panico[4] as follows:

---

[4] This example is taken from Panico, *op. cit.*, pp. 55–58.

TABLE 6–1

Actual Data of Shipments

	Lockages[a]	Straight Throughs[b]
January	49	221
February	104	175
March	26	343
April	13	361
May	457	16
June	497	0
July	504	0
August	591	0
September	606	0
October	455	0
November	439	6
December	426	0
	4167	1122

[a]"Lockages" means that the boats and barges must be elevated or lowered by the lock to continue on their way.
[b]"Straight Throughs" describes the condition of "open river" in which barges go over the top of the dam because the river has been elevated owing to heavy rains or snow.
Source: Panico, Joseph A. *Queuing Theory.* Englewood Cliffs, N.J.: Prentice-Hall, 1969.

Arrival Times

Boats may approach the dam from opposite directions, but the first come–first served rule still holds. The total number of boats processed by the dam is somewhat cyclical due to river conditions and seasonal characteristics of the industries receiving materials by water. These data, as given, do not follow a Poisson distribution, so it must be reexpressed with respect to another time period. A sampling of hourly boat arrivals resulted in a Poisson distribution that allowed the data from Table [6–1] to be utilized.

The data for May through December were used to find the mean arrival time because they better describe the use of the dam and its locks. Furthermore, these data were used as an approximation of the queues developing the period January through April. The fact that the river is relatively slow in rising or falling means that the lockages occur in groups for January and April, and that the queues that form follow, somewhat, the patterns found during the months of heavy usage.

Service Times

Numerous studies were made to determine the service time since no records were available giving these data. Service time was found to be exponentially distributed with a mean servicing time of 40 minutes.

With these data it is possible to solve for E_n (the expected number of boats in the system), E_w (the expected number of boats waiting service). This information is extremely important both to the owners of the boat and to the U.S. Corps of Engineers. An exceptionally long waiting time represents for the owners lost opportunity of business and poor equipment utilization. Consider also how these costs may compound as a boat travels through numerous dams from the embarkation to destination points. To the Corps of Engineers, waiting time increases river congestion because more boats are needed to move materials and there is a heavier concentration of boats around the dam.

Solution

Utilizing the data May through December, the lock-ages = 3975 boats. Total number of 24-hour days = 245, total hours = 5880. Thus

$$\text{Arrivals (boats/hr)} = \frac{3975}{5880} = 0.676 \text{ (boats arriving for service per hour}$$

$$\text{Lockage (service time)} = 40 \text{ min or } \frac{60 \text{ min}}{40 \text{ min}} = 1.5$$

$$\text{(average number of boats serviced per hour}$$

Therefore

$a = 0.676/\text{hr}$

$s = 1.500/\text{hr}$

$P = \dfrac{0.676}{1.500} = 0.451$

$P < 1$ which satisfies the restriction that $\dfrac{a}{s} < 1$

$$E_n = \frac{a}{s-a} = \frac{0.676}{1.500-0.676} = 0.820 \text{ boats (being serviced plus waiting)}$$

$$E_w = \frac{a^2}{s(s-a)} = \frac{0.457}{1.5(0.824)} = \frac{0.457}{1.2360} = 0.370 \text{ boats (waiting service)}$$

$$E_t = \frac{E_w}{a} = \frac{0.370}{0.676} = 0.547 \text{ hr} \quad \text{(time boat can expect to wait before being serviced)}$$

TABLE 6–2

Probabilities of Arrivals

n	$P_n(t)$[a]	$P(N > n) = (a/s) n + 1$[b]
0	$1 - a/s = 0.549$	$0.451 = 0.451$
1	$P_0(t) (0.451)^1 = 0.248$	$(0.451)^2 = 0.203$
2[c]	$P_0(t) (0.451)^2 = 0.112$	$(0.451)^3 = 0.092$
3	$P_0(t) (0.451)^3 = 0.050$	$(0.451)^4 = 0.041$
4	$P_0(t) (0.451)^4 = 0.023$	$(0.451)^5 = 0.019$
5	$P_0(t) (0.451)^5 = 0.010$	$(0.451)^6 = 0.008$
6	$P_0(t) (0.451)^6 = 0.005$	$(0.451)^7 = 0.004$

[a]$P_0(t)$ = a barge has the probability $P_0(t)$ = 0.549 of being immediately processed, $P_1(t)$ = 0.248 of being the only barge awaiting service, $P_2(t)$ = 0.112 of being second in line, etc. (given the first come–first served discipline).
[b]$P(N > n) = (a/s)^{n+1}$ shows the complement of the cumulative probabilities line size will be greater than $0 = (1 - 0.549) = 0.451$, $Pr(N > n)$, (greater than 1) = $1 - (0.549 + 0.248) = 0.203$.
[c]A boat captain could reason that the probabilities of exactly one boat's being processed, and one waiting, when he arrived at the dam equaled 0.112, but the probabilities that there would be more than two $P(N > 2) = 0.092$; with these odds he would have an exceptionally good chance of meeting his delivery date.
Source: Panico, Joseph A. *Queuing Theory*. Englewood Cliffs, N.J.: Prentice-Hall, 1969.

Table [6–2] gives the probabilities for various n's. When $n = 2$,

$$P_2(t) = 0.112 \quad \text{and} \quad P(N > 2) = 0.092$$

The differences between two successive $P(N > n)$ values is equal to the individual P_n.

Thus the probability that there will be exactly two units in the system is equal to: *Pr* (there is more than one unit in the system) minus *Pr* (there are more than two units in the system) or

$$P_2(t) = P(N > 1) - P(N > 2) = 0.112$$

Mathematically this is expressed as

$$\left(1 - \frac{a}{s}\right)\left(\frac{a}{s}\right)^2 = \left(\frac{a}{s}\right)^2 - \left(\frac{a}{s}\right)^3 = 0.112$$

From the $P(N > n)$ column in Table [6–2] it is seen that for 9 percent of the time, more than two boats are waiting for service. If this is acceptable both to the owners and to the Corps of Engineers, then the present system is sufficient.

Cost Analysis

One boat represents a cost to the owners of \$226/hr. Thus, if it passes through six dams in one day, the waiting cost will be

$$\frac{6 \text{ trips}}{\text{day}} \times \frac{0.547 \text{ hr}}{\text{trip}} \times \frac{\$226}{\text{hr}} = 6 \times (E_t) \times (\$226) = 6 \times 0.547 \times \$226$$
$$= \$742 \text{ (cost of waiting per day)}$$

Conclusion

Knowledge of waiting time will unquestionably aid the engineer in future designing projects and will also draw attention to the present problems. If the current situation is causing too much congestion and lost time, the engineers may theoretically change the values of s to find an output rate to relieve the problem. A change in s would mean faster pumps, more crew at the lock, improved methods of reducing crew-servicing time, faster gates, etc. If these were not economical, then new dams or more locks could be recommended.

A forecast of river traffic for the next few years may show an anticipated 40 percent traffic increase with much larger and faster boat-barge combinations.[5] The calculations of an increase in boat traffic of 40 percent are

$$a = \frac{3975 + .40(3975)}{5880} = 0.946/\text{hr}$$

$$s = 1.5/\text{hr}$$

$$E_n = \frac{a}{a - a} = \frac{0.946}{1.5 - 0.946} = 1.708 \text{ boats (being serviced plus waiting)}$$

$$E_w = \frac{a^2}{s(s - a)} = \frac{0.946^2}{1.5(1.5 - 0.946)} = \frac{0.895}{0.831} = 1.075$$

$$E_t = \frac{E_w}{a} = \frac{1.075}{0.946} = 1.136 \text{ hr} \quad \text{(time boat can expect to wait before being serviced)}$$

Applying the same cost of \$226 per hour and passing through six dams in one day, the total waiting cost per day is

$$(6) \times (1.136) \times (\$226) = \$1540$$

---

[5] Panico, *op. cit.*, pp. 55–58.

The new waiting cost would show an increase of 108 percent [($1540 − $742)/$742]. The boat owners can analyze the expected increase in costs relative to the effect upon profits as a basis for decision making. One possible course of action would be to increase freight rates.

SIMULATION APPROACH

The simulation approach differs from the statistical method described above in that it does not involve collection of empirical data. Simulation analysis is based upon the use of synthetic data such as random numbers generated in the Monte Carlo technique. Random numbers may be obtained from a list of such numbers or they may be generated by a computer. The simulation approach is less time consuming and less expensive. It is also more flexible since the analyst has control of the process and can experiment with it, which makes simulation a useful approach in the investigation of complex queuing problems. There are also instances in which the computation method is not applicable: (1) when it is impossible to collect empirical data in a given situation, (2) when empirical data is confidential, and (3) when empirical data is not standardized because of different sources of supply.

A key consideration limiting use of the simulation approach is the questionable validity of the original model as a true representation of the relevant universe. If the original model is filled with personal bias, the results are bound to be biased. Reference is made to the Dreyfus method of analysis in which the French General Staff used science to convict Captain Alfred Dreyfus of treason. The majority of scientists in the case considered Captain Dreyfus innocent, but the Army's investigators would only accept those scientific proofs that supported their predetermined beliefs. Therefore scientific analysis was the basis for acceptance of an incorrect hypothesis.[6] This condition represents a possible bias in the analysis of business problems.

Example of Simulation Approach

The simulation approach in a Monte Carlo format can be applied to waiting-line problems with minimum information available. One example is analysis of the efficiency of a supermarket checkout station. Arrival of customers per minute would fit the model of a Poisson distribution. The analyst would need to know what the average number of arrivals is in order to simulate the distribution. Past experience can be

---

[6] *Ibid.*, p. 135.

used as a basis for estimation; in this case, assume that the average number is one arrival per minute. Calculation of probabilities of arrivals over time is shown by solving the formula for a Poisson distribution:

$$P_{(k)} = \frac{m^k}{k_!} e^{-m}$$

where k is the number of arrivals being considered $(0,1,2, \ldots ,n)$, e is the base of the natural logarithms and is equal to 2.71828, and m is the average number of arrivals. For zero arrivals

$$P_0 = \frac{1^0}{0_!} (2.71828)^{-1} = 0.37$$

The full complement of computations is shown as

Number of Arrivals in a Minute	Probability
0	0.37
1	0.37
2	0.18
3	0.06
4	0.02

To simulate probable arrivals, the analyst can establish a relationship between probability and random numbers so that zero number of arrivals is determined by a random number in the range 01–37 to conform to the probability of 0.37 for zero arrivals. Likewise one arrival per minute is determined by a random number in the range 38–74; two arrivals per minute by a random number in the range 93–98; and four arrivals per minute by a random number in the range 99–00. The analyst can simulate the arrivals per minute for a full day by generating 480 numbers (60 minutes × 8 hours = 480 minutes). The number of arrivals per minute would be determined in the simulation by the relationship to the numbers above. For example, a random number with a value of 93–98 would simulate three arrivals for that minute of the day. A significant consideration is the need to avoid bias in the method of generating random numbers in the analysis.

Another aspect of the problem is the service rate. The analyst would have past experience as a guide to average service time. The application would then be to simulate expected service time according to designated random numbers. Assume that the service rate is found to be as follows:

Service Time in Minutes	Probability	Random Numbers
1	0.30	01–31
2	0.40	32–71
3	0.20	72–91
4	0.10	91–00

Random numbers are generated to simulate service rate for each arrival. Starting with the first arrival, the random number generated to simulate the service time for it will simulate the time required to service completely the first arrival. For example, if the random number is 37, it falls in the range for service time to be 2 minutes. The same procedure is repeated for all arrivals. An analysis of the simulated situation will disclose such results as the average length of line and average wait in line. A manager can then determine the desirability of the simulated results.

EMPIRICAL EXAMPLE OF SIMULATION APPROACH[7]

During winter months, workers in one department complain constantly about the cold air that blows on them whenever their overhead door is used by fork-truck drivers. The situation magnifies, as door usage increases, to the extent that many workers leave their machines whenever the door is opened. Productivity suffers and this unquestionably disturbs management. The door is finally placed on a 1-minute time-delay relay system, with positive safety features that operate automatically as trucks use the doors. This reduces time through the door as drivers no longer must quit their vehicles to operate the door switches, and it also eliminates the spiteful lingering for a long while as the machine operators complain.

This solution only relieves the individual situation, for again with the increased usage the department is cold. Heating and ventilating engineers recommend the use of an air lock, which uses two doors automatically timed so that one truck requires 2 minutes through the system. This will stop the cold

---

[7] *Ibid.,* pp. 139–143.

blast of air and save fuel, but will delay trucks since only one can use this door system at one time. A suggestion from one of the workers in the department recommends that an air door, similar to those doors made of air in department stores, be installed so that this will give free entrance and exits without delay or discomfort to the workers.

Investigations reveal that use of this door is extremely heavy and that the trucks cannot be sent along another route since this would result in a considerable delay.

Analysis

An analysis of truck arrival times is found to have the following probability distribution shown in Table [6–3].

TABLE 6–3

Truck Arrival Times

Minutes Between Arrivals	Probability	Monte Carlo Numbers
0	0.028	001–028
1	0.201	029–229
2	0.267	230–496
3	0.226	497–722
4	0.160	723–882
5	0.075	883–957
6	0.026	958–983
7	0.010	984–993
8	0.005	994–998
9	0.001	999
10	0.001	000

Source: Panico, Joseph A. *Queuing Theory*. Englewood Cliffs, N.J.: Prentice-Hall, 1969.

To simulate this process it is essential that: (a) Input and output data be shown in terms of a probability distribution, given that enough observations have been made to assure reliability; (b) the probability distribution be expressed as random numbers; (c) columns be set up to depict how one element passes through the system in a chosen unit time; and (d) enough individual experiments are conducted to assure reliability.

TABLE 6–4

Simulation of Trucks Through Proposed Air Lock

Random Number	Minutes Between Arrivals	Time Truck Arrives at Door	Minutes Truck Waits	Truck Through Door	Minutes Door Not Utilized
186	1	1	1	4	0
914	5	6	0	8	2
120	1	7	1	10	0
142	1	8	2	12	0
776	4	12	0	14	0
564	3	15	0	17	1
013	0	15	2	19	0
978	6	21	0	23	2
694	3	24	0	26	1
074	1	25	1	28	0
029	1	26	2	30	0
072	1	27	3	32	0
962	6	33	0	35	1
748	4	37	0	39	2
920	5	42	0	44	3
097	1	43	1	46	0
539	3	46	0	48	0
337	2	48	0	50	0
299	2	50	0	52	0
020	0	50	2	54	0
723	4	54	0	56	0
685	3	57	0	59	1
421	2	59	0	61	0
544	3	62	0	64	1
530	3	65	0	67	1
158	1	66	1	69	0
997	8	74	0	76	5
358	2	76	0	78	0
219	1	77	1	80	0
692	3	80	0	82	0
809	4	84	0	86	2
Totals	84		17		22

Source: Panico, Joseph A. *Queuing Theory.* Englewood Cliffs, N.J.: Prentice-Hall, 1969.

In Table [6–4] the simulation begins with one truck in the air lock. This first line reads, "The number 186 taken from the random-number table shows 1 minute elapsed between this arrival and its immediate predecessor. This truck cannot be immediately processed because there is another truck in the air lock requiring an additional minute of servicing time. The incoming truck must therefore wait 1 minute until its servicing commences. After servicing, the truck departs at time-block four having spent 3 minutes in the system; the air lock was completely utilized during this first sample. Additional examples show: (a) At time-block 15, two trucks arrive simultaneously; (b) time-block 42 indicates that the door is not utilized for 3 minutes because it was empty at time-block 39 minutes without any demand for service until the 42nd minute; and (c) a truck requires service during the 27th minute but cannot be accepted into the system until 3 minutes later because the door is not cleared until that time and also because other trucks are before it, given a first come–first served discipline regardless of which side of the door is approached.

84/31 – 2.70968 min (average arrival time), 17/31 = 0.54838 min (average waiting time per truck)
22/31 – 0.70967 min (average lost servicing opportunity) 22 min

From the 31 randomly selected numbers shown in Table [6–4], 84 minutes transpired, 17 minutes of waiting time were required for 31 trucks, and the door was not used for 22 minutes. These data, however, are far from being representative as they have not been simulated through enough trials. To give some idea how this varies, two individual trials of 67 experiments were conducted with the following results:

Number of Experiments	Minutes Between Arrivals	Truck Waiting Time	Minutes Door Not Utilized	Average Arrival Time (min)	Average Waiting Time (min)	Average Lost Servicing Opportunity (min)
67	197	25	61	2.94	0.373	0.910
67	176	34	42	2.63	0.507	0.627
134	373	59	103	2.78	0.440	0.769

These two trials vary considerably, which shows that there is a great probability of obtaining biased results if the sample size is too small; if, however, this total sample size of 134 trials were adequate, then a cost analysis could be undertaken.

Cost data

Engineers have calculated: The average cost to reheat air for seven months of use = $0.250/opening; cost of air-lock system = $12,500 ($8000 door plus installation, and $4500 for space costs); cost of air door = $37,500; days of use per year = 152; truck cost per hour = $9.73 (includes lost opportunity).

Cost Analysis Air Lock (Three Shifts 24-Hour Day)

a. $\dfrac{24 \text{ hr}}{\text{day}} \times \dfrac{60 \text{ min}}{1 \text{ hr}} \times \dfrac{1 \text{ arrival}}{2.78 \text{ min}} = \dfrac{517.32 \text{ arrivals}}{\text{day}}$

b. $\dfrac{517.32 \text{ arrivals}}{\text{day}} \times \dfrac{0.44 \text{ min waiting}}{\text{arrival}} \times \dfrac{1 \text{ hr}}{60 \text{ min}} =$

$$\dfrac{3.79 \text{ hr of waiting}}{\text{day}}$$

c. Process time $= 2 \text{ min} \times \dfrac{\text{hr}}{60 \text{ min}} \times \dfrac{517.32 \text{ arrivals}}{\text{day}} =$

$$\dfrac{17.24 \text{ hr}}{\text{day}}$$

d. Cost of service $= \dfrac{\$9.73}{\text{hr}} \times \dfrac{17.24 \text{ hr}}{\text{day}} = \dfrac{\$167.75}{\text{day}}$

e. Cost of waiting $= \dfrac{\$9.73}{\text{hr}} \times \dfrac{3.79 \text{ hr of waiting}}{\text{day}} = \dfrac{\$36.88}{\text{day}}$

f. Total cost $= \dfrac{36.88 + 167.75}{\text{day}} = \dfrac{\$204.63}{\text{day}}$

g. Average yearly cost (152 days) $= \dfrac{\$31,103.76}{\text{yr}}$

Conclusion

In the actual situation management did not adopt either the air-lock or air-door system even though the present system resulted in an exceptionally high fuel cost. This is not unusual, since requests for moneys usually exceed what is available. Management must therefore give up a desirable program, much

TABLE 6–5

A Comparison of the Two Proposals

Cost of Facility		Air Lock	Air Door
		$12,500	$37,500[a]
Waiting time	(517.32) (0.44/60)	3.79 hr/day	0[b]
Processing time	(517.32) (2/60)	17.24 hr/day	0
Waiting cost	(9.73) (3.79)	$36.88	0
Servicing cost	(9.73) (17.24)	$167.75	0
Total daily cost	(36.88 + 167.75)	$204.63	0
Days system used		152/yr	152/yr
Total service cost	(204.63) (152)	$31,103.76/yr	0

[a]The cost of the air door could be justified solely from the total service cost of the air lock versus air door if the slightly higher costs of maintaining an air door were disregarded.
[b]This table shows that there is zero cost for truck processing through an air-door system. Theoretically there is that rare possibility of demand being so heavy, in one time period, that some waiting will occur. This is very small, and costs are minimal. Air doors when improperly designed for traffic can also present some waiting time, but not in this situation.
Source: Panico, Joseph A. *Queuing Theory.* Englewood Cliffs, N.J.: Prentice-Hall, 1969.

like an individual who must pass up an exceptional value in mink coats when his resources meet only the basic needs for sustenance.[8]

_____

[8] *Ibid.*, pp. 139–143.

CHAPTER 7

Simulation

Simulation is a powerful problem-solving technique. A useful working definition of a simulation model is "a representation of some real system or operation (such as the market for a given product) which is sufficiently realistic in its structure and content to be used to determine the effects of a complex set of input conditions on the system."[1] Given a problem, a manager is able to portray a complex system by the use of the simulation approach, to test the impact of alternative actions, and to select the "best" solution.

CIRCUMSTANCES FOR USE OF SIMULATION MODELS

Simulation studies are particularly useful in three types of studies: (1) in situations that contain a complicated set of interrelated variables, (2) in situations in which there is uncertainty, and (3) in situations in which costs of an analytical approach would be prohibitive. In the instance of complex situations, analytical models usually require simplifying assumptions and do not produce effective results. For example, a study of advertising effectiveness by an analytical model (such as regression analysis) does not test either cause and effect relationships or the simultaneous influence of variables on one another as would a simulation model. A simulation model can be designed not only to test a complex situation but, in addition, after repeated runs may come close to an optimum solution. It was not until the advent of computers that decision makers could utilize the simulation technique in an effective manner, since a computer provides rapid analysis of complex situations.

---

[1] Frank, Ronald E., and Green, Paul E. *Quantitative Methods in Marketing.* Englewood Cliffs, N.J.: Prentice-Hall, 1967 (p. 82).

In fact, simulation models are often called computer models.[2] A disadvantage is that simulation cannot guarantee an optimum solution as is possible with an analytical model.

Another situation in which simulation is useful is one in which uncertainty exists. For example, simulation can be used to experiment with new situations for which little or no information is available. The first use of the simulation technique is credited to von Neumann and Ulam in their pioneering research to solve certain nuclear-shielding problems.[3] As a note of caution, care must be taken that the simulation model is a reasonably accurate structure of the real situation. Analytical models have checkpoints because of assumed distribution; however, such checkpoints are not available in those simulation models that have characteristics of uncertainty. One might obtain simulation results that look reasonable in terms of the model, but fall short of representing the real process.

A third situation in which simulation is applicable occurs when use of an analytical approach would be prohibitively costly. Analytical studies involving real-life investigations, such as physical sampling of population or products, have a combination of factors of time, resources, and product loss which could add up to an expense unwarranted by the potential payoff. However, a simulation study of the same problem situation can substitute computer-generated processes in place of the physical investigation, thereby reducing research costs to an acceptable level. Care must be taken in generating computer data so as not to bias the analysis. The avoidance of bias is probably the most difficult problem in simulation analysis.

General to all the three situations for use of simulation analysis are the following reasons:[4]

1. Simulation makes it possible to study and experiment with the complex internal interactions of a given system whether it be a firm, an industry, an economy, or some subsystem of one of these.
2. Through simulation one can study the effects of certain informational, organizational, and environmental changes in the operation of a system by making alterations in the model of the system and observing the effects of these alterations on the system's behavior.

---

[2] Spencer, Milton H., and Siegelman, Louis. *Managerial Economics*. Homewood, Ill.: Richard D. Irwin, 1959 (p. 529).

[3] Naylor, Thomas H. *et al. Computer Simulation Techniques*. New York: Wiley, 1968 (p. 1).

[4] Naylor, *op. cit.,* pp. 8, 9.

3. Detailed observation of the system being simulated may lead to a better understanding of the system and two suggestions for improving it, which otherwise would not be obtainable. "There is indeed a good deal of evidence that human beings have a great capacity for understanding the workings of complicated systems, and can find near optimum decision rules, operating procedures, etc., if they have enough experience with the system and it is stable enough."

4. Simulation can be used as a pedagogical device for teaching both students and practitioners basic skills in theoretical analysis, statistical analysis, and decision making. Among the disciplines in which simulation has been used successfully for this purpose include business administration, economics, medicine, and law.

5. Operational gaming "has been found to be an excellent means of stimulating interest and understanding on the part of the participant, and is particularly useful in the orientation of persons who are experienced in the subject of the game."

6. The experience of designing a computer simulation model may be more valuable than the actual simulation itself. The knowledge obtained in designing a simulation study frequently suggests changes in the system being simulated. The effects of these changes can then be tested via simulation before implementing them on the actual system.

7. Simulation of complex systems can yield valuable insight into which variables are more important than others in the system and how these variables interact.

8. Simulation can be used to experiment with new situations about which we have little or no information so as to prepare for what may happen.

9. Simulation can serve as a "preservice test" to try out new policies and decision rules for operating a system, before running the risk of experimenting on the real system.

10. "Simulations are sometimes valuable in that they afford a convenient way of breaking down a complicated system into subsystems, each of which may then be modeled by an analyst or team which is expert in that area."

11. For certain types of stochastic problems the sequence of events may be of particular importance. Information about expected values and moments may not be sufficient to

describe the process. In these cases Monte Carlo methods may be the only satisfactory way of providing the required information.

12. Monte Carlo simulations can be performed to verify analytic solutions.

13. Simulation enables one to study dynamic systems in either real time, compressed time, or expanded time.

14. When new components are introduced into a system, simulation can be used to help foresee bottlenecks and other problems that may arise in the operation of the system.

15. "Simulation makes generalists out of specialists. Analysts are forced into an appreciation and understanding of all facets of the system, with the result that conclusions are less apt to be biased by particular inclinations and less apt to be unworkable within the system framework."

Managers should recognize that there are limitations in the use of simulation models: (1) computer simulation may be expensive, primarily because of the computer time required; (2) computer system-design problems posed by a simulation can be extremely complex; (3) data input procedures must be designed with considerable care so that they will not subsequently inhibit ones ability to use the model for experimental purposes; and (4) it is often difficult to develop adequate tests of the validity of the overall simulation model or its components.[5] In any given situation, the manager should consider the possible shortcomings of simulation analysis.

CLASSIFICATION

Simulation models can be classified as follows:[6]

1. Purpose
   (a) Prognostic models
   (b) Process of behavioral models
2. Degree of System Definition
   (a) Tactical models
   (b) Strategic models

[5] Frank and Green, *op. cit.,* p. 88.

[6] Weitz, Harold. The promise of simulation in marketing. *Journal of Marketing*, 31(July, 1967): 29.

3. Structural Characteristics
  (a) Static–dynamic models
  (b) Deterministic–stochastic models
  (c) Aggregative–disaggregate models

Prognostic models are concerned with output, or the results of the model computation, for predictive purposes, whereas process or behavioral models are concerned with relationships of the model variables in order to formulate theories to describe that behavior.

Tactical models are concerned with the effect of alternative values or actions within a given structure. An example of the type of question asked in tactical models is what is the impact of changing one of the elements of marketing mix for a given product in an existing market? In strategic models the concern is to develop a model about some elements and relationships about which little is understood, such as consumer behavior. The objective is then to test continually and revise the model until ultimately it is a valid basis for prediction.

Static models involve an instant of time, like a snapshot, whereas dynamic models cover a period of time like a movie; deterministic models include absolute values whereas stochastic models are based on probabilistic values; and aggregative models are a study of a complete system whereas disaggregate models are studies of subsystems—for example, a particular segment of consumers for a product.

These various classifications of simulation models may be developed by different processes. The type of model to be utilized will depend on the particular need in a problem situation. The following section presents the Monte Carlo process, heuristic programming, and experimental gaming as examples of different possible simulation models.

Monte Carlo Technique

The Monte Carlo method is the approach most often used in simulation studies. Monte Carlo is essentially a stochastic approach, in which random numbers are generated by a computer to represent the makeup of a problem similar to what would be expected in the real world. Basis for the random selection is usually empirical data that describe the problem situation. It should be clear that any bias in the generating of random numbers by the computer would seriously bias the analysis and the results of the model.

Conceptual process. A manager can model a given universe by assigning random numbers to empirical knowledge about the different proportions involved. Consumers, for example, could be represented according to buying behavior so that if 25 percent were loyal to brand A, random digits 00 to 24 could be labeled to represent that group. In the generation of random numbers, any selection of 00 to 24 would be interpreted as a consumer who would be a loyal buyer of brand A. The remaining 75 percent of consumers would be assigned random numbers from 25 to 99 according to empirical proportions. Continuous generation of random numbers would simulate the problem situation, leading to probable results—a replication of real-life events.

Marketing research example. A marketing research manager wishes to institute field procedures that will minimize field research costs.[7] One specific problem is a choice between two alternative schedules:

A. An interviewing schedule of six hours per day, with three hours before six o'clock and three hours after, or

B. An interviewing schedule of three hours per day, with interviews in the evening only.

One basis for the decision is management judgment. The manager can assume that the probability of respondents being at home is much higher in alternative B, resulting in a larger percentage of completed interviews. However, costs will be increased in alternative B, because the travel from origin to destination is spread over fewer hours of productive interviewing. It would seem that alternative B is better than alternative A, but judgment alone is not sufficient to evaluate the relationship of these plus and minus cost considerations for the manager to make a sound decision.

Another possible approach to the study of this problem is an analytical model. Constraints of time, cost, and the structure of the field force precluded the use of the analytical approach in this situation.

Application of a Monte Carlo model is suitable in this problem situation. Empirical data were available from the Survey Research Center of the University of Michigan on which to simulate the interviewing environment. The center had compiled data on the results of approximately 3000 attempted interviews. There were three alternative responses from the interview call: Selected interviewees may not have been at home, may have refused to cooperate, or may have granted the interview. The pattern of interviewer behavior in these empirical data is a basis for simulating probable responses in a planned interview study.

---

[7] The example is taken from the article by Mayer, Charles S. Pretesting field interviewing costs through simulation. *Journal of Marketing*, 28(April, 1964): 47–50.

The actual simulation procedure was carried out as follows:

1. The computer selected a respondent based on a subroutine that considered distance from the interviewer and the possible choices.
2. The computer recorded the time necessary for the interviewer to reach the respondent.
3. The computer determined the result of the call (not at home, no cooperation, or completed interview). The basis for this determination was the relevant probabilities for each respondent to which the computer generated a random number and interpreted it as to the outcome of that call. For example, "The computer may recognize that this is the third call in a rural area made on Monday through Friday before 6:00 P.M. and that the respondent was not home on the last call. The relevant probability number under these circumstances is 0.42. The computer then generates a random number, say 0.214, and in this case interprets the result as a completed interview. Had the random number been greater than 0.42, it would be interpreted as either a terminal or a nonterminal noninterview."[8]
4. The computer recorded the result of the call and the time required to complete the call.
5. The computer decided whether time remained to make another call. If so, a new respondent was selected and the cycle repeated. If time was not available for another call, passage of one day was recorded and the process repeated under the conditions indicated on a new day.

Use of the simulation model provided a quick and definitive answer to the manager's problem. Where judgment could not determine a sound basis for choice, use of the Monte Carlo method generated results that indicated not only the better alternative, but also a measure of the difference. Alternative A was superior to alternative B, costing 40 percent less.

Inventory control example. An excellent application of Monte Carlo simulation is in the field of inventory control. Following is an example in which a manager must determine an appropriate number of floor polishers to inventory for his rental service.[9] One factor for consideration is the irregular demand for his floor polishers. His records indicate the probability for 5 units to be ordered in one day is 0.150; for 10 units, it is 0.250; for 15 units, it is 0.450; and for 20 units, the probability is 0.150. So the first step in designing the simulation model is to describe the

---

[8] *Ibid.*, p. 49.

[9] This example is based on material in text by Clark, William A., and Sexton, Donald E. *Marketing and Management Science.* Homewood, Ill.: Richard D. Irwin, 1970 (pp. 365–367).

interpretation of random numbers generated by a computer as follows:

If the Number Drawn Is	This Many Polishers Are Ordered
000–149	5
150–399	10
400–849	15
850–999	20

Records also indicate that there is a likelihood of 1 out of 60 that a polisher will require maintenance, which takes three days. So, added to the model would be 60 random numbers: 00 to 59, to simulate maintenance need. This procedure provides a basis for the computer to check possible maintenance needs of each unit by drawing a random number from the group of 60 numbers. For purposes of the model, if a number from 00 to 58 is drawn, then that polisher is considered operative. If the number 59 is drawn, then that unit would be considered inoperative and kept out of circulation in the model for the three days required for maintenance.

The manager can simulate quickly the probable daily demand for rental polishers and maintenance need for a period of years by having a computer generate random numbers in pairs. The first number indicates the quantity ordered and the second indicates the maintenance need. The analysis thus provides the manager with an answer to the problem of what is the optimum inventory level for the business.

Profit evaluation for new product introduction example. A relevant application of the Monte Carlo simulation technique is in the problem of determining the profit potential of introducing a new product. There is insufficient data available to structure the problem, so an analytical solution is not possible. However, it is possible to assign probability values to the fundamental variables in the problem and then to simulate a reasonable solution.

In one example of new product evaluation, the simulation approach incorporated consideration of four factors: (1) price, (2) sales volume, (3) investment, and (4) cost and expense.[10] These factors are interrelated in an equation to yield return on investment (ROI),

$$\text{ROI} = \frac{(\text{price} \times \text{volume}) - (\text{cost} + \text{expenses})}{\text{fixed investment} + \text{working capital}} \times 100$$

A manager or management team must determine what level of profit-

[10] This example is based on material from the text by Clark and Sexton, *op. cit.,* pp. 368–372.

ability should be the goal; assume it is 15 percent in this example. Although absolute values are missing, subjective values can be assigned to the various elements in the problem. First, probable estimates by marketing personnel for the price of the new product ranged form 25 to 40 cents; the forecasters were 90 percent sure that the price should be 30 to 35 cents, have a 6 percent probability that the price should be 25 to 30 cents, and were 4 percent sure that the best price would be 30 to 35 cents. By assigning random numbers to this situation, a computer can be utilized in the following manner:

If the Machine Draws	The Price Forecast Is (cents)
00–05	25–29.99
06–95	30–34.99
96–99	35–40

A similar probability distribution is developed for the other three variables of volume, investment, and cost and expense, based on estimates and probabilities given by appropriate specialists. Then the computer is used to generate random numbers for each of the four variables. A return on investment is calculated for each series of draws according to the equation given earlier. The process is repeated many times until the simulation results indicate an estimated pattern of occurrence as shown in Figure 7–1. A decision maker can use the results as a basis for analyzing probable success of the new product. The distribution does show that the most likely return on investment would be 15 percent. Since this result agrees with the announced profit goal, the decision could be a "green light" for the new product.

The simulation model indicates a definite element of risk that return on investment could be less than the desired 15 percent. Management may wish to investigate the problem more closely before making a decision. The analysis could be revised to include a greater effort in the procedure to determine probabilities associated with the original four variables. For example, marketing research studies may be undertaken to obtain better data about price acceptance and sales volume. Subsequent simulation operations could conceivably change the shape of the results. If the curve is more concentrated around 15 percent or more, the decision maker can be more confident in making a positive decision. It is clear that probability estimates of problem variables such as price, volume, investment, and cost and expense are of significant importance in the use of simulation models in new product decisions.

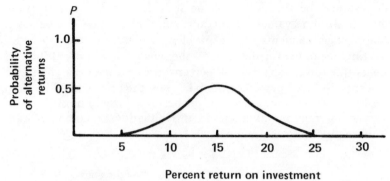

Figure 7–1.   Simulated return on investment

Heuristic Programming

Another type of simulation model is heuristic programming, which has as its objective "the reproduction of decision processes as developed by human problem solvers."[11] In this technique the manager does not limit his program to numerical processes; he also includes ideas from the less systematic, more selective, processes that humans use in handling problems. Instead of seeking an optimal solution, a manager applying heuristic programming is seeking a satisfactory solution consistent with the cost of developing better alternatives.

Heuristic programming is applicable to any management problem for which a sequence of steps for solution can be identified. A flow diagram that illustrates an example of heuristic programming is as follows:

---

[11] Frank and Green, *op. cit.,* p. 95.

The procedure does not include any mathematical computations, but rather recognizes fundamental factors that must be considered in the problem. For this reason managers find that heuristic programming lends itself to solving those many types of problems that are not well structured and thus unsuitable for analytical models.

Conceptual process. Heuristic programming is basically a simple concept, a rule of thumb used to solve a particular problem. Business managers use heuristics quite often in making fairly routine decisions. A rule of thumb in job scheduling, for instance, could be first come, first served. Such a heuristic frees a decision maker from solving the same or similar problems over and over again. The simple rule may not lead to an optimum solution each time, but it is accepted as a satisfactory and efficient procedure. By some sophisticated extensions to heuristic programming, combined with the use of a computer, a manager can handle many problems that are not practical to solve with analytical methods.

The actual procedure in heuristic programs is well explained by J. D. Weist as follows:

> Most business-oriented heuristic programs apply to what has been characterized as combinatorial problems because of the extremely large number of ways in which a series of decisions can be made. A problem may be likened to a maze consisting of a sequence of decision points; at each point a number of paths are available but only one can be chosen. Figure [7–2] illustrates the process.
>
> There are numerous combinations of paths which lead from the initial point to some terminal point. A series of 10 decision points, each of which could be made in five different ways, leads to almost 10,000,000 combinations of decisions ($5^{10} = 9,765,625$). The heuristic technique is to prune the combinations of paths that appear to be of doubtful value. There is a risk that the pruning process may eliminate a path that leads to the optimum solution. That is the trade-off for reaching at least a satisfactory solution, when the cost of reaching an optimum solution, with linear programming for example, is prohibitive.[12]

Application to problem of locating warehouses. An outstanding example of the usefulness of heuristic programming is in the geograph-

---

[12] Weist, Jerome D. Heuristic program for decision making. *Harvard Business Review,* 44 (September–October, 1966): 131–132.

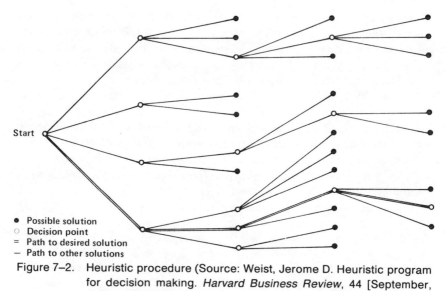

Start

● Possible solution
○ Decision point
= Path to desired solution
— Path to other solutions

Figure 7–2. Heuristic procedure (Source: Weist, Jerome D. Heuristic program for decision making. *Harvard Business Review*, 44 [September, 1966]: 131–132)

ical pattern determination "of warehouse locations which would be most profitable to the company by equating the marginal cost of warehouse operation with the transportation cost savings and incremental profits resulting from more rapid delivery."[13]

The heuristic program is made up of two parts: (1) the main program and (2) the bump and shift routine. In the main program, warehouses are added one at a time until an additional warehouse will increase total costs to a point at which marginal cost would exceed marginal revenue. After processing in the main program is done, the bump and shift routine examines the solution for possible modification, primarily to eliminate warehouses that are not economical because customers originally served by them were being serviced more efficiently by warehouses that were added later.

The principal heuristics used in the main program are as follows:

1. Most geographic locations are not promising sites for a regional warehouse; locations with promise will be at or near concentrations of demand. The use of this heuristic permits concentration on less than

---

[13] Example is based upon the article by Kuehn, Alfred A., and Hamburger, Michael J. A heuristic program for locating warehouses. *Management Science*, 9(July, 1963): 643–666.

1/100 of 1 percent of the total land area of the United States as a basis for possible locations.
2. Near optimum warehousing systems can be developed by locating warehouses one at a time, adding at each stage of the analysis that warehouse which produces the greatest cost savings for the entire system. The use of this heuristic reduces the time and effort expended in evaluating patterns of warehouse sites.
3. Only a small subset of all possible warehouse locations need be evaluated in detail at each stage of the analysis to determine the next warehouse site to be added. The N potential warehouse sites chosen at each stage are those which, considering only local demand, would result in the greatest cost savings (or smallest increase in costs) if serviced by a local warehouse rather than by the system existing in the previous stage. In other words it is assumed that at any stage we can do reasonably well by locating the next warehouse in one of the N areas chosen on the basis of local demand and related warehousing and transportation costs.

A flow diagram for warehouse location is shown in Figure 7–3. Steps 4, 5, and 7 indicate that the program either eliminates the site from further consideration, assigns a warehouse to that location, or returns the location to the list of potential warehouse sites for reconsideration at later stages in the program. When the list of potential warehouses is depleted, all sites having been either eliminated or assigned a warehouse, the program enters the bump and shift routine as shown in step 8 of the flow diagram.

The results of the study suggest that a heuristic approach to the warehouse-location problem may be quite profitable in practice. At the time, the authors were examining two actual warehouse network problems, one representing the distribution of a variety of grocery–drug type consumer products, the other a line of consumer appliances.

Application to portfolio selection. In the next example we have a program written to simulate decision-making activities of a particular trust investment officer in his selection of a portfolio, based on information available to him at the time he makes a decision.[14] The following characteristics are included in the program:

1. A preference list of stocks is established and stored in the computer memory. This list, designed to cover various economic conditions and updated periodically by the officer, is taken as a given in the program.

---

[14] Clarkson, Geoffrey P., and Meltzer, Allan H. Portfolio selection: A heuristic approach. *Journal of Finance*, 15(December, 1960): 465.

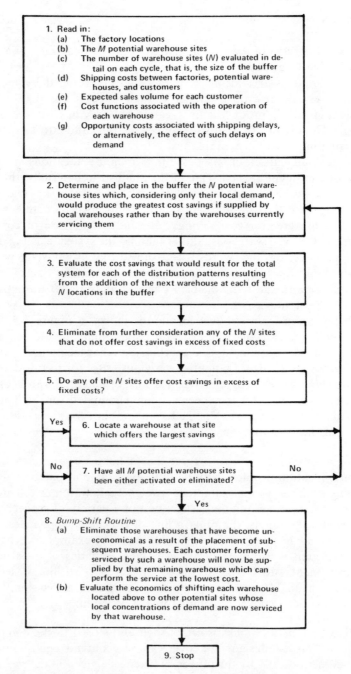

Figure 7–3.   (Source: Kuehn, Alfred, and Hamburger, Michael, A heuristic program for locating warehouses. *Journal of Marketing*, 9 [July, 1963]: 647.)

2. Various data associated with each of the companies represented in the list are also stored.
3. From this list a portfolio is generated, based on heuristics that relate information about the client, the securities market, and the economy to the selection of particular stocks in the list. The heuristics were compiled from a study of past decisions of the trust officer and verbalizations of his decision processes.
4. The program keeps a record of its past decisions and their outcomes and modifies its future behavior by eliminating unsuccessful procedures. Thus the program "learns" from its previous experience —paralleling to some extent human learning processes.

Application to assembly line balancing.[15] Given a manufacturing process involving a progressive assembly line, it is possible to apply heuristic programming in determining the division of assembly work among the operators, a problem of "line balancing." For the most part enumeration techniques, which are usually used to tackle the problem, result in industry wastes of 4 to 10 percent of operators' time on assembly lines through unequal work assignments. Analytical approaches to the problem prove to be overwhelmingly complicated. Therefore a heuristic method is desirable.

Procedure for a heuristic technique in assembly line balancing is as follows:

The work is divided into a given number of operators of equal duration while heeding necessary sequential restrictions. Each operation consists of one or more irreducible work elements combined in such a way as to equalize the time required for each operation.

A precedence diagram is drawn so that the assembly progresses from left to right, each element being as far left as possible at the start of the procedure. First, in column I of the diagram are listed all work elements which need not follow any work elements. Then in column K (K II) are entered all those work elements which must follow work elements already on the diagram. Finally arrows are drawn from work elements in column K–1 to work elements in column K which must follow them. This procedure is repeated, replacing column K–1 by columns K–2, . . . ,1, successively, except that no arrow is drawn

---

[15] This example is based on the article by Kilbridge, Maurice, and Wester, Leon. A heuristic method of assembly line balancing. *Journal of Industrial Engineering*, 12(July–August, 1961): 292–298.

from one work element to another, if it is possible to follow arrows already drawn from the first work element to the second.

The problem of line balancing is to achieve the least possible balance delay (amount of idle time on the line due to the imperfect division of work between stations) for given conditions. Thus for a specified distribution of elements and restriction on their ordering, and a given cycle time, c, one may be required to find the minimum number, n, of operators to perform the task; or for a given number, n, of operators, one may wish to determine the shortest cycle time, c. If neither c nor n is given, it is necessary to determine the value, or values, of c and n for which balance delay is zero.[16]

Guidelines for the application of the heuristic method described above are as follows:

1. Permutability within columns is used to facilitate the selection of elements of the length desired for optimum packing of the work stations. Lateral transferability helps to deploy the work elements along the stations of the assembly line so they can be used where they best serve the packing solution.

2. Generally the solutions are not unique. Elements assigned to a station, which belong after the assignment is made in one column of the precedence diagram, can generally be permuted within the column. This allows the line supervisor some leeway to alter the sequence of work elements without disturbing optimum balance.

3. Long time elements are best disposed of first, if possible. Thus, if there is a choice between the assignment of an element of duration, say, 20, and the assignment of two elements of duration, say, 10 each, assign the larger element first. Small elements are saved for ease of manipulation at the end of the line.

    The situation is analogous to that of a paymaster dispensing the week's earnings in cash. He will count out the largest bills first. Thus, if the amount to be paid a worker is $77, the paymaster will give three $20 bills first, then one $10 bill, one $5 bill, and two $1 bills, in that order.

---

[16] *Ibid.,* pp. 294–295.

4. When moving elements laterally, the move is best made only as far to the right as necessary to allow a sufficient choice of elements for the work station being considered.[17]

Experiment Gaming

Experimental gaming is another type of simulation. Its purpose can be stated as follows: "To test in an artificial environment certain hypotheses about human behavior that, because of the complexity of the real world and the difficulty of control, cannot easily be tested under ongoing conditions."[18] This objective is differentiated from business gaming, which has as its purpose use as an educational tool for training managers.

Conceptual process. A group of people are placed in a situation that simulates a real environmental pattern. The experimenter varies characteristics of the simulated situation to test human behavior. The manner in which the test group responds to changes is observed and recorded. It is believed that results of experimental gaming will lead to some generalizations about human behavior. The important factor as emphasized by E. Pessemier is that the experimental conditions should be psychologically equivalent to a real life situation, although physical identity is not necessary.[19] He suggests the following procedure in order to encourage subjects in an experimental environment to act in the same manner they would on real shopping trips.

First, subjects should be asked to make selections from normal assortments of brands presented in a graphic form that display the characteristics of the merchandise. Second, each subject should be given a personal "stake" in acting according to *his own* system of values relating to the various products and in expressing them in monetary terms.

Each individual can be asked to assume that he needs an item from each of several classifications and that he has enough money to "purchase" any item from each classification. Further, he can be told that each set of assortments which he will see represents what is available in the market at the time, and that he should select the items he would choose under similar real shopping conditions.

To encourage normal behavior, he should be informed

---

[17] *Ibid.,* p. 298.

[18] Frank and Green, *op. cit.,* p. 100.

[19] Pessemier, Edgar A. Forecasting brand performance through simulation experiments. *Journal of Marketing,* 28(April, 1964): 41.

TABLE 7–1

Brand Market Shares During Simulated Shopping Trips Following Selected Price Increases
in Subject's Preferred Brand-Toothpaste Classification

Tooth-paste Brands	Percentage of Subjects Originally Preferring a Brand	Percentage of All Subjects Selecting a Designated Brand When the Price of the Brand Normally Preferred by Each Subject Was Increased		
		1¢	3¢	5¢
A	33.8	33.8	31.3	28.4
B	29.7	27.8	24.4	20.0
C	17.2	17.1	20.6	21.3
D	8.4	8.5	10.6	13.1
E	7.2	8.4	8.4	10.3
F	3.7	4.1	4.4	6.3
G		.3	.3	.6
Total	100.0	100.0	100.0	100.0

Source: Pessemier, Edgar A. Forecasting brand performance through simulation experiments. *Journal of Marketing*, 28 (April, 1964): 42.

that he will *actually receive the merchandise and change* called
for by his purchase decisions on several of the simulated
shopping trips made during the series of experiments.[20]

Application to consumer behavior and price change.[21] In one study the
investigator engaged 320 adults in a shopping experiment to test the
effect of price change on toothpaste and soap. The subjects were given
money to purchase merchandise in the experiment and were allowed to
keep the products that had been selected. On successive simulated
shopping trips, the price of the brand normally preferred by the
individual in each classification would be raised, or the price of a
nonpreferred brand lowered. Consumer behavior was recorded and a
sample of results is shown in Table 7–1.

A manager can thus develop some data concerning how price
changes would affect consumer demand for his brand and for competing
brands. Prior to making a decision involving a change in price, a
manager can use experimental results to forecast the parallel change in
sales and profit. These data normally are difficult to obtain in the real
market, primarily due to the lack of control any one manager has over
the dynamic variables in a market environment.

[20] *Ibid.*, p. 21.
[21] This application is based on the study in Pessemier, *op. cit.*, pp. 41–42.

Future of simulation models. From all indications there will be increased use of simulation models in business decision making. As problems become more complex and analytical techniques become correspondingly less appropriate, managers will become more and more dependent on simulation techniques for satisfactory results. In addition, managers must be concerned with countervailing actions in their decision environment. It is important to program possible reactions by competitors as a part of the problem solution. Analytical models are limited in accounting for these characteristics whereas simulation models are very appropriate. Finally, factor relationships in an environment tend to change over time. Analytical models are not suited for these dynamic solutions whereas simulation models can be designed to include such changes.

In general, simulation models are useful when an analytical solution is not possible or when difficulties and costs make use of the latter prohibitive. It should be remembered, however, that analytical models have the capability of producing an optimal solution whereas simulation models are associated with approximation solutions.

CHAPTER 8

Markov Chains

INTRODUCTION

The Markov chain process, named after the Russian mathematician Andrei Markov (1856–1922), is a quantitative technique useful for analyzing trends. It is particularly useful as a means of examining and forecasting consumer loyalty, market stability, investment decisions, and price changing. Unlike probability theory in which each outcome involves independent events, the outcome of an event in the Markov process is dependent on the result of preceding events. Markov processes are classified into "orders" according to the number of event outcomes under consideration; in the first-order Markov process, the outcome of an event depends on the outcome of the single preceding event. Empirical research has indicated that many behavioralistic processes do appear to exhibit properties of this assumption.[1] There are higher-order Markov processes that can be used for models in which it is assumed that more than the last preceding event outcome influences the trend; however, the rest of this chapter will be limited to only the first-order Markov process.

STATES, TRANSITION PROBABILITIES, AND TRANSITION MATRIX

A Markov process contains (1) outcomes, which are called "states," and (2) transition probabilities. Typically the process is shown in the form of a matrix as follows:

---

[1] Alderson, Wroe, and Green, Paul E. *Planning and Problem Solving in Marketing.* Homewood, Ill.: Richard D. Irwin, 1964 (p. 181).

	a_1	a_2
a_1	P_{11}	P_{12}
a_2	P_{21}	P_{22}

The states are represented by a_1 and a_2, and the transition probabilities are shown by the numbers p_{11}, p_{12}, p_{21}, and p_{22}. For example, a highly simplified model of trends in consumer behavior patterns can be shown in the transition matrix:

$$P =$$

	A	B
A	0.7	0.3
B	0.2	0.8

Conditions of the model are as follows:

1. Probability of consumer repeat purchase of Company A's product is 0.7 and for switching to a competitive brand is 0.3. It is not necessary to assume that the same consumers will always be in the same perference group every time.
2. Consumer preference for all competitive products is shown by probabilities of 0.8 for repeat purchases and 0.2 for brand switching. All competitive products are grouped for simplification of computation. Realistically each competitive product would have a distinctive consumer preference.

THE PROBABILITY TREE

The Markov process can also be shown by a probability tree diagram as in Figure 8–1.

The probability tree illustrates three steps in the process with the letters M_A and M_B indicating the market shares of products A and B; the numbers in the subsequent stages are the probabilities for change from one state to another.

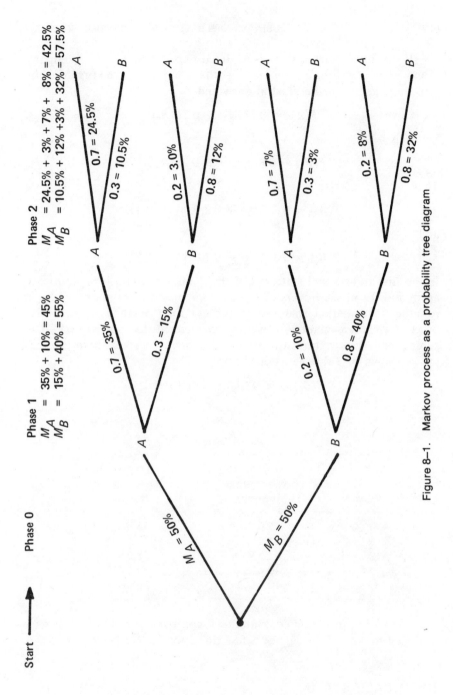

Start →

Phase 0

Phase 1
M_A = 35% + 10% = 45%
M_B = 15% + 40% = 55%

Phase 2
M_A = 24.5% + 3% + 7% + 8% = 42.5%
M_B = 10.5% + 12% + 3% + 32% = 57.5%

M_A = 50%

M_B = 50%

0.7 = 35%

0.3 = 15%

0.2 = 10%

0.8 = 40%

0.7 = 24.5%

0.3 = 10.5%

0.2 = 3.0%

0.8 = 12%

0.7 = 7%

0.3 = 3%

0.2 = 8%

0.8 = 32%

Figure 8–1. Markov process as a probability tree diagram

111

If the initial market share is assumed to be 50 percent for Company A and 50 percent for all others (B, all other companies), the first Markov transitional state in the illustration would be

$$P(A)_1 = 0.7P(A_0) + 0.2P(B_0)$$

Similarly,

$$P(B_n) = 0.8P(B_{n-1}) + 0.3P(A_{n-1})$$

Then

$$P(A_n) = 0.7(0.50) + 0.2(0.50) = 0.45$$

and

$$P(B_n) = 0.8(0.50) + 0.3(0.50) = 0.55$$

In the first transitional state, 0.7 of the A buyers would buy product A again and 0.2 of the buyers of competitors' products would switch to A resulting in a market share of 45 percent for Company A. A similar process yields a market share of 55 percent for the others. The subsequent Markov transitional states involving market share changes are as shown in Table 8.1. For example,

$$P(A_2) = 0.7P(A_1) + 2P(B_1) \text{ etc.}$$

TABLE 8–1

Market Shares

Period	Company A's Market Share (percent)	All Others' (B) Market Share (percent)
1	45.0	55.0
2	42.5	57.5
3	41.25	58.75
4	40.625	59.375
5	40.3125	59.6875

The period-to-period computational approach in Table 8–1 shows a tendency to stabilize after just a few transition states.

THE STEADY STATE

Consumer preferences will pass through transitional phases shown by the Markov process and eventually reach an equilibrium state known

as the "steady state," assuming, of course, that the probability relationships remain constant. (Later we will see how marketing strategy is
applied to effect a change in the probability relationships of consumer
brand switching behavior.) In Table 8–1 we can perceive the stabilization
of the market shares. From a practical standpoint it is believed that a
steady state is reached by the time of the second transition state after the
competitive environment undergoes some sort of change,[2] such as
introduction of a new promotional campaign by a competitor.

The steady state can be computed in a direct manner to determine
the new market shares of competing firms. In the preceding problem the
original transition probability matrix can be written in the following
equation form:

$$A = 0.70A + 0.20B$$
$$B = 0.30A + 0.80B$$

In addition, we have $A + B = 1$, since the sum of the final market
shares must total 100 percent. The resulting system of equations can be
solved simultaneously for A and B, showing that the market share for A
in the steady state is 40 percent and for B is 60 percent.

An important property of the steady state is that these final
equilibrium probabilities are *independent* of the starting point (market
shares of 50 percent for both A and B in the above example) and depend
solely on the transition probabilities. An illustration will show this
property. In the above example the transition matrix is

		A	B
		A	**B**
A		0.7	0.3
B		0.2	0.8

$p =$

and the initial starting point is given by the vector

$$p^{(0)} = \begin{bmatrix} 0.5 & 0.5 \end{bmatrix}$$

The vector $p^{(1)}$ gives the probability of states A and B after one stage by
the vector product

$$p^{(1)} = p^{(0)}P = \begin{bmatrix} 0.5 & 0.5 \end{bmatrix} \begin{bmatrix} 0.7 & 0.3 \\ 0.2 & 0.8 \end{bmatrix}$$
$$= \begin{bmatrix} 0.35 + 0.1 & 0.15 + 0.4 \end{bmatrix} = \begin{bmatrix} 0.45 & 0.55 \end{bmatrix}$$

---

[2] *Ibid.*, p. 186.

Continuing,

$$p^2 = p^{(1)}P = \begin{bmatrix} 0.45 & 0.55 \end{bmatrix} \begin{bmatrix} 0.7 & 0.3 \\ 0.2 & 0.8 \end{bmatrix} = \begin{bmatrix} 0.315 + 0.11 & 0.135 + 0.44 \end{bmatrix}$$

$$= \begin{bmatrix} 0.425 & 0.575 \end{bmatrix}$$

Thus the associative law holds,

$$p^{(2)} = p^{(1)}P = (p^{(0)}P)P = p^{(0)}P^2$$

This process may be carried on for any number (t) of trials and it may readily be seen that where $p^{(t)}$ is the probability vector over the states A and B after t stages,

$$p^{(t)} = p^{(0)}P^{(t)}$$

This has the important consequence that P^t is the matrix for the transition from A_i to A_j in t stages; that is, the ijth entry is the probability of moving from A_i to A_j in t steps just as is shown by the two-stage development

$$P^2 = \begin{bmatrix} 0.7 & 0.3 \\ 0.2 & 0.8 \end{bmatrix} \begin{bmatrix} 0.7 & 0.3 \\ 0.2 & 0.8 \end{bmatrix}$$

$$= \begin{bmatrix} (0.7)(0.7) + (0.3)(0.2) & (0.7)(0.3) + (0.3)(0.8) \\ (0.2)(0.7) + (0.8)(0.2) & (0.2)(0.3) + (0.8)(0.8) \end{bmatrix} = \begin{bmatrix} 0.55 & 0.45 \\ 0.30 & 0.70 \end{bmatrix}$$

$$p^{(2)} = p^{(0)}P = \begin{bmatrix} 0.5 & 0.5 \end{bmatrix} \begin{bmatrix} 0.55 & 0.45 \\ 0.30 & 0.70 \end{bmatrix} = \begin{bmatrix} 0.275 + 0.15 & 0.225 + 0.35 \end{bmatrix}$$

$$= \begin{bmatrix} 0.425 & 0.575 \end{bmatrix}$$

which is the same result as was computed above in two steps. It would be possible to take t successive stages of P and arrive at the steady state of $A = 0.40$ and $B = 0.60$ as computed by simultaneous equations, so that the transition matrix is in equilibrium.

	A	B
A	0.40	0.60
B	0.40	0.60

Although there will be individual shifting taking place, the net effect in the matrix will remain the same:

$$\begin{bmatrix} 0.40 & 0.60 \\ 0.40 & 0.60 \end{bmatrix} \begin{bmatrix} 0.40 & 0.60 \\ 0.40 & 0.60 \end{bmatrix} = \begin{bmatrix} 0.40 & 0.60 \\ 0.40 & 0.60 \end{bmatrix}$$

APPLICATION OF THE MARKOV PROCESS

Computation of a steady state competitive situation illustrates brand loyalties by the diagonal probabilities in the matrix and brand switching by the probabilities off the diagonal. The analysis will indicate to managers the degree of customer loyalty to their products and to competitors' products, and will also indicate to whom they are losing customers and from whom they are gaining customers.

In practice the dynamic feature of business operations precludes a transition matrix from reaching a steady state. Managers should actually be attempting to change the transition probabilities more to their advantage by means of one strategy or another. Changes in the transition probabilities should not, however, discourage managers from utilizing the Markov process in analysis. At any given time a current transition matrix (1) will point out the direction in which market shares are moving and (2) will provide short-term forecasts of market-share positions. Both of these conclusions are beneficial for executive decision making.

COST-BENEFIT ANALYSIS

Business executives can apply the Markov process to analyze two types of problem situations. First there is the consideration of evaluating the potential payoff benefit of a cost input. A firm typically is interested in profit maximization, so that a cost input can be regarded as marginal cost to be compared to resulting marginal revenue. For example, the possibility of a special promotion to influence consumer demand can be cast in a Markov process framework. In the preceding problem example the equilibrium state had Company *A* at 40 percent and the other firms in the industry at 60 percent and the consumer preferences were

From	To	
	A	Others
A	0.7	0.3
Others	0.2	0.8

Company *A* executives can evaluate a proposed advertising campaign of $500,000 against the probable effect on consumer preference and profits. A market test involving the proposed advertising schedule could be conducted in a sample area. Marketing research in the sample area, perhaps utilizing the consumer panel approach, would measure the resulting effects of the advertising on consumer brand switching. Assume that the pilot advertising campaign changed consumer preferences so that the new matrix is

From	To	
	A	Others (B)
A	0.8	0.2
Others (B)	0.3	0.7

The new equilibrium state would show that Company A now has 60 percent of the market whereas the rest of the industry has 40 percent. This net increase of 20 percent (40 percent to 60 percent) in market share to Company A can be converted to an equivalent sales and profit increase to be considered as the marginal revenue effected by the marginal cost of $500,000; all other factors are assumed to have remained constant. Company A executives would have a tangible cost-benefit analysis upon which to evaluate the potential payoff of the proposed advertising program. (Obviously the executives would have to incorporate the present value concept in their analysis because of the time lag between the start of the campaign and the stimulated shift to a new equilibrium state.)

The Markov process is also useful in analyzing the repercussions of a competitor's strategy. Assume that Company A had decided to conduct the $500,000 campaign. Competitors' executives, having observed the new strategy, can also collect data through marketing research to determine the change in consumer preferences. Their loss of sales and profit to Company A can be measured, providing competitors with information upon which to consider consequent action, for example, to conduct a counter-offensive strategy to Company A's campaign.

Case Study Applied to Marketing[3]

A survey of 100 households was made with housewives reporting their purchase of laundry cleaning products in a weekly diary for 26 weeks. This information was categorized into states of a Markov analysis as follows:

1. Family buying detergent only
2. Family buying soap powder only
3. Family buying both detergent and soap powder together
4. Family buying no laundry powder at all

[3] Material is based on Styan, G. P. H., and Smith, H., Jr. *Markov Processes Applied to Marketing* (unpublished paper).

Frequency data for the four states were found to be fairly steady and transition matrices were set up for each of the purchase periods. Each transition matrix was considered to define a Markov process and when tested statistically, found to be of first order (dependent on preceding periods) rather than zero order (or a random process). In addition, statistical tests of the 25 transition matrices supported the hypothesis that they were based on some unique underlying matrix, which was considered to define a stationary Markov process.

The stationary matrix was analyzed and a steady state situation computed to show buying patterns as follows:

	(percent)
1. Detergents only	23
2. Soap only	37
3. Detergents and soap	10
4. Neither	30

These results provide a basis for management to predict changes in consumer purchases. The average purchases in the test period of 26 weeks was

	(percent)
1. Detergents only	21
2. Soap only	41
3. Detergents and soap	7
4. Neither	31

Therefore it can be seen that family purchases will shift in a predictable fashion. A manager can expect that the number of families purchasing detergents only should increase 2 percent, the number purchasing soap only should decrease 4 percent, the number purchasing detergents and soap should increase 3 percent, and the number purchasing neither should decrease 1 percent. A conclusion of the study was that the use of Markov processes in marketing has thus been shown to be very useful as a predictive device.

Application to Investment Decisions

The use of Markov analysis is a forward-looking approach, which is beneficial in investment decision making. Analysis of transition matrices indicates the trend of probable future sales based on the dynamics of shifting brand preferences in Markov chains. For example,[4] an invest-

---

[4] Massy, W. F., and Morrison, D. G. Comments on Ehrenberg's appraisal of brand-switching models. *Journal of Marketing Research*, 5(May, 1968): 227.

ment service erred on one occasion by recommending purchase of Ford stock, partly because Ford's market share at the time was approximately 25 percent instead of the company's historic market share of 28 to 30 percent, which the service concluded meant that Ford sales should rise. The service had assumed that Ford's market share in the steady state was 28 to 30 percent. On the contrary an analysis of the transition matrix for automobile sales indicated that Ford's long-run brand share (assuming purchasers maintained the same switching patterns) was only 22 percent. The movement of Ford automobile sales was downward and not upward as the investment service had concluded. The service would be well advised to compute a Markov steady state in their analytical procedure for the purpose of determining probable change.

Application to Pricing

An established business concern can apply the Markov chain process to predict the effect of a price change on volume of sales. An example of this application is the pricing plan by a wholesale house[5] that had been experiencing declining sales because of competition from limited-line discount wholesalers and price conscious retailers, who were the consumers. In an effort to improve his position, the wholesaler considered a revision of his pricing structure as shown in Table 8–2.

TABLE 8–2

Total Monthly Sales	Present Discount (average percentage)	Proposed Discount (percent)
Under $4000	3.21	No change
$4000–$6000	3.74	5.0
$6000–$8000	4.46	6.5
Over $8000	3.35	8.0

The first step of the Markov analysis was to summarize current accounts into 13 classes as shown in Table 8–3. Each salesman was then asked to predict probable customer reaction to the pricing change. A summary of salesmen's predictions is shown in the transition probability matrix of wholesaler customers in Figure 8–2. The diagonal values in this probability matrix indicate the "no change" consumers, whereas the

[5] Blumenthal, P. L. Predicting sales effects of discount changes. *Management Advisors*, 8(March–April, 1971): 37.

Number of customers	Group	0 (out)	1	2	3	4	5	6	7	8	9	10	11	12	summary
0	0 (New)	0*	0	0	0	0	0	0	0	0	0	0	0	0	0
107	1	0.052	0.887*	0.005	0.009	0.005	0	0.027	0.005	0.005	0	0.005	0	0	1.00
105	2	0.02	0	0.84*	0.01	0.03	0.031	0.04	0.01	0.02	0	0	0	0	1.00
133	3	0.02	0	0.01	0.76*	0	0.05	0.16	0.01	0.01	0	0.01	0	0	1.00
65	4	0	0	0	0	0.62*	0.02	0.26	0.03	0.03	0.01	0.03	0	0	1.00
41	5	0	0	0	0	0	0.52*	0.27	0	0.18	0	0.02	0	0	1.00
18	6	0.05	0	0	0	0	0	0.70*	0	0.20	0	0.05	0	0	1.00
11	7	0	0	0	0	0	0	0	0.43*	0.27	0	0.30	0	0	1.00
10	8	0	0	0	0	0	0	0	0	0.70*	0	0.23	0	0.08	1.00
1	9	0	0	0	0	0	0	0	0	0	0.25*	0.50	0	0.25	1.00
2	10	0	0	0	0	0	0	0	0	0	0	0.88*	0	0.12	1.00
0	11	0	0	0	0	0	0	0	0	0	0	0	0*	0	0
3	12	0	0	0	0	0	0	0	0	0	0	0	0	1.00*	1.00
496															

*diagonal

Figure 8–2. Transition probability matrix of wholesaler customers

119

values to the right indicate a shift to a higher-volume class and the values to the left indicate a shift to a lower class (salesmen predicted that they would lose some of those customers who could not easily qualify for savings in the next pricing schedule).

TABLE 8–3

Group	Monthly Volume (dollar)	Number of Customers February, 1970
0	None (used for new customers coming into the system or old ones dropping out)	
1	1– 500	107
2	501– 1000	105
3	1001– 2000	133
4	2001– 3000	65
5	3001– 4000	41
6	4001– 5000	18
7	5001– 6000	11
8	6001– 7000	10
9	7001– 8000	1
10	8001– 9000	2
11	9001–10000	0
12	Over 10000	3
	Total	496

The next step in the Markov process is to determine a steady state of customers classified into the four-part pricing policy as shown in Table 8–4.

TABLE 8–4

Total Monthly Sales (dollar)	Proposed Discount (percent)	Percent of Customers
Under $4000	No change	X_1
$4000–under $6000	5.0	X_2
$6000–under $8000	6.5	X_3
$8000 and over	8.0	X_4

Computation of probable monthly sales based on the steady state of consumer purchasing pattern would provide management with a measuring stick which to evaluate the proposed pricing change. Prior to accepting the change, management would be in a position to compute expected payoff results affected by the price change. If the Markov analysis yields a larger expected payoff than previous experience, then a change, such as the proposed change in pricing structure is desirable.

ASSUMPTIONS IN THE MARKOV CHAIN MODEL

Underlying the theory of the Markov process are some assumptions that should be understood. One assumption is that the probability of a particular transition is based on the most recent phase, independent of earlier history. As indicated in the introduction to this chapter, many behavioral processes exhibit properties of this assumption. In other instances if the difference between the model and the behavioral process is not too great, the model is useful for making meaningful predictions.

A second assumption is that the consumers all purchase the same quantities of the product being studied and all have the same transitional probability in each given state. In practice, the Markov analysis could be structured to separate differentiated classes of consumers and thus avoid possible bias. In one instance consumers can be placed into such categories as large quantity purchasers and small quantity purchasers. Regarding the transition probability, consumers can be categorized as different groups, for example, strong loyalty versus weak loyalty.

In the case of each of the above assumptions, it is possible to redefine the states in the Markov process in order to overcome possible limitations.

CHAPTER 9

Regression and Correlation Analysis

INTRODUCTION

Regression analysis and correlation analysis are effective tools in the decision-making process. These analyses inform the manager of the relationships that exist between the variable factors in predictive and control problems. Regression analysis is a statistical technique for developing a model in which a dependent variable, Y, is estimated from one or more independent variables, X. Such a model is used in sales forecasting to forecast the demand for new cars based on such factors as disposable personal income, number of family units, and highway mileage.

Correlation analysis can supplement regression analysis by determining the closeness of the relationship between two or more variables, citing the variation in the dependent variable explained by the independent variable(s) in the analysis. Although no attempt should be made to infer cause and effect relationships between the variables, correlation analysis does indicate the percentage change in the dependent variable that is associated with variations in the independent variables, such as change in new car sales related to change in disposable personal income. This additional analysis improves the basis for such decisions as sales forecasting. Regression and correlation analyses are usually implemented as a single procedure in order for the analyst to obtain maximum benefit.

SIMPLE REGRESSION

When a problem contains only two variables, the statistical analysis is called "simple regression." A first step in simple-regression analysis is the plotting of a scatter diagram from sample data relevant to the problem. In the illustration of forecasting new car sales, data collected for the number of new cars purchased in the United States and the disposable personal income in the United States for the years 1951–1970, as shown in Table 9–1, are plotted in a scatter diagram (Figure 9–1).

TABLE 9–1

New Car Sales and Disposable Personal Income In the United States

Year	New Car Sales (in millions of units) (X)	Disposable Personal Income (in billions of dollars) (Y)
1951	5.3	227.5
1952	4.3	238.7
1953	6.1	252.5
1954	5.6	256.9
1955	8.0	274.4
1956	5.9	292.9
1957	6.4	308.8
1958	4.7	317.9
1959	6.3	337.3
1960	7.2	350.0
1961	5.8	364.7
1962	7.3	384.6
1963	8.0	402.5
1964	8.3	438.1
1965	9.7	473.2
1966	9.2	508.8
1967	8.1	546.3
1968	10.4	591.2
1969	10.0	631.6
1970	8.5	684.8

Source: U.S. Department of Commerce. *Statistical Abstract of the United States.* Washington, D.C.: U.S. Government Printing Office, 1972; and *Automobile Facts and Figures.* Detroit, Mich.: Automobile Manufacturing Association, 1972.

Visual examination of the scatter diagram will indicate the degree of relationship between the dependent and independent variables as fitting into one of three models of relationship shown in Figure 9–2.

Examination of the scatter diagram will also indicate the type of relationship between the variables, for example, linear versus curvilinear.

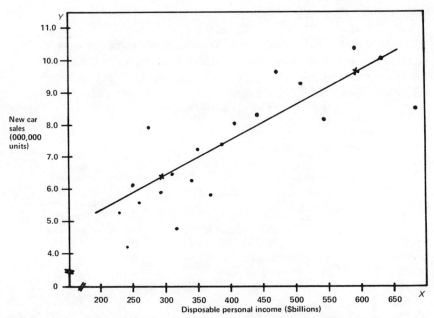

Figure 9–1.   Scatter diagram of new car sales and disposable personal income (Source: U.S. Department of Commerce, *Statistical Abstract of the United States*. Washington, D.C.: U.S. Government Printing Office, 1972; and *Automobile Facts and Figures*. Detroit: Automobile Manufacturing Association, 1972)

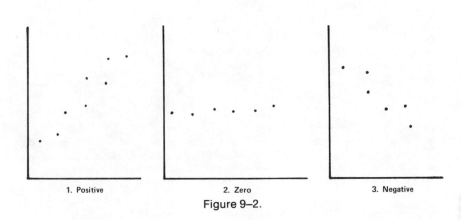

Figure 9–2.

124

This observation is helpful in the computation of the regression equation. In some instances a freehand approximation of the regression line can be drawn on the scatter diagram, giving a quick answer to a problem or a preliminary result as a "go—no go" phase preparatory to conducting sophisticated analysis of the data. The freehand regression line should be drawn so that about half of the points are above the line and half below. Given a certain value for the independent variable, disposable personal income, it would be possible to estimate the dependent variable, new car sales, from the graph. An equation for the regression line can be estimated from the freehand line by utilizing coordinates of any two points and applying them in the formula for a straight line,[1]

$$Y_c = Y_1 + \frac{Y_2 - Y_1}{X_2 - X_1}(X - X_1)$$

Then the analyst could compute the value of the dependent variable by entering the value of the independent variable in the equation.

Use of Least Squares Analysis

The method of least squares is a statistical technique that determines mathematically the straight line which is the best fit to the variables in a regression analysis. The least squares line is called the "best fit" because of its mathematical properties: (1) The sum of the differences of the actual values and the computed values for the independent variables is equal to zero and (2) the sum of the squares of the differences about the least squares line is smaller than the sum of the differences about any other straight line through the given values.

Certain assumptions must be met in order to make inferences about population relationships from regression analyses based on sample data. These assumptions are as follows:

1. The population relationship of variables must be linear if the regression analysis of sample data is based on a linear relationship.
2. There is a uniform scatter or dispersion of points around the regression line.
3. The deviation of one point about the regression line is unrelated to the deviation of any other point.
4. The distribution of points above and below the line follows a roughly normal curve.[2]

[1] See Spencer, Milton, and Siegelman, Louis. *Managerial Economics*. Homewood, Ill.: R. D. Irwin, 1964 (p. 133) for a detailed explanation.

[2] Spurr, William, and Bonini, Charles. *Statistical Analysis for Business Decisions*. Homewood, Ill.: R. D. Irwin, 1967 (p. 564).

Computation of Least Squares Line

Determination of the regression equation that yields the line of best fit to sample data is accomplished by solving normal equations. There are two normal equations needed to solve for a straight line (one for each constant to be determined in the equation $Y = a + bX$). The procedure for finding the normal equations[3] is as follows:

1. The first normal equation is found by multiplying the straight-line equation through by the coefficient of the first constant and then summing. The first constant is a and its coefficient is 1. Multiplying through by 1 does not change the equation: $Y = a + bX$. Summing the equation,

$$\Sigma(Y = a + bX) = \Sigma Y = na + b\Sigma X$$

which is the first normal equation.
2. The second normal equation is found by multiplying the straight-line equation through by the coefficient of the second constant and then summing. The second constant is b and its coefficient is X. Multiplying through by X results in

$$XY = aX + bX^2$$

Summing yields

$$\Sigma(XY = aX + bX^2) = \Sigma XY = a\Sigma X + b\Sigma X^2$$

which is the second normal equation.

The normal equations are applied to the illustration of new car sales to determine the least squares line as follows: New car sales data are considered dependent (Y variable) on disposable personal income (X variable). The calculation, with values found in Table 9–2, is

$$\Sigma Y = na + b\Sigma X$$
$$\Sigma XY = a\Sigma X + b\Sigma X^2$$
$$145.1 = 20a + b\,7882.7$$
$$61{,}010.2 = a\,7882.7 + b\,3{,}465{,}810$$

Simultaneous solution of the normal equations yields $a = 3.08$ and $b = 0.0106$. Substituting in the straight-line equation for the least squares line,

$$Y_c = 3.08 + .0106X$$

Thus having an estimate of the single independent variable of disposable personal income, X, the manager can compute Y_c to predict new car sales. If disposable personal income is estimated to be $300 billion in a

---

[3] Richmond, Samuel B. *Statistical Analysis*. New York: Ronald Press, 1964 (pp. 356, 357).

certain year, by substituting in the above equation, sales would be forecasted as

$$Y_c = 3.08 + 0.0106(300)$$

or 6.24 million cars. For an estimate of $600 billion disposable personal income, the forecast would be 9.44 million cars. The entire least squares line is shown in Figure 9–1 drawn through the two computed points.

The Standard Error of Estimate

The standard error of estimate is a mathematical measurement of the goodness of fit of the least squares line to the empirical data in the

TABLE 9–2

Relationship Between New Car Sales and Disposable Personal Income

	New Car Sales (in millions of units) Y	Disposable Personal Income (in billions of dollars) X	XY	X^2	Y_c	$Y\text{-}Y_c$	$(Y\text{-}Y_c)^2$
1951	5.3	227.5	1,205.75	51,756.25	5.49	−0.19	0.0361
1952	4.3	238.7	1,026.41	56,977.69	5.61	−1.31	1.7161
1953	6.1	252.5	1,540.25	63,756.25	5.76	0.34	0.1156
1954	5.6	256.9	1,438.64	65,997.61	5.80	−0.20	0.0400
1955	8.0	274.4	2,195.20	75,295.36	5.99	2.01	4.0400
1956	5.9	292.9	1,728.11	85,790.41	6.18	−0.28	0.0784
1957	6.4	308.8	1,976.32	95,357.44	6.35	0.05	0.0025
1958	4.7	317.9	1,494.13	101,060.41	6.45	−1.75	3.0625
1959	6.3	337.3	2,124.99	113,771.29	6.66	−0.36	0.1296
1960	7.2	350.0	2,520.00	122,500.00	6.79	0.41	0.1681
1961	5.8	364.7	2,115.26	133,006.09	6.95	−1.15	1.3225
1962	7.3	384.6	2,807.58	147,917.16	7.16	0.14	0.0196
1963	8.0	402.5	3,220.00	162,066.25	7.35	0.65	0.4225
1964	8.3	438.1	3,636.23	191,931.61	7.72	0.58	0.3364
1965	9.7	473.2	4,590.04	223,918.24	8.09	1.61	2.5921
1966	9.2	508.8	4,680.96	258,877.44	8.47	0.73	0.5329
1967	8.1	546.3	4,425.03	298,443.69	8.87	−0.76	0.5776
1968	10.4	591.2	6,148.48	349,517.44	9.35	1.05	1.1025
1969	10.0	631.6	6,316.00	398,918.56	9.77	0.23	0.0529
1970	8.5	684.8	5,820.80	468,951.04	10.34	−1.84	3.3856
Sum	145.1	7,882.7	61,010.18	3,465,810.23			19.7335

Source: U.S. Department of Commerce. *Statistical Abstract of the United States.* Washington, D.C.: U.S. Government Printing Office, 1972; and *Automobile Facts and Figures.* Detroit, Mich.: Automobile Manufacturing Association, 1972.

problem. If the differences of the empirical data and the least squares line are normally distributed, then 68 percent of the differences should be within a distance of one standard error of estimate from the line as shown in Figure 9–3. Then 95.5 percent of the difference should be within a distance of two standard errors of estimate from the line and 99.7 percent of the differences should be within a distance of three standard errors of estimate from the line.

The computation of the standard error of estimate is

$$S_{Y \cdot x} = \sqrt{\frac{\Sigma(Y - Y_c)^2}{n}}$$

Substituting the values from Table 9–2,

$$S_{Y \cdot x} = \sqrt{\frac{19.7335}{20}} = 0.99$$

This means that the analyst has 68 percent confidence that the range of $Y_c \pm 0.99$ will include the actual value. In a business situation the range of $Y_c \pm 2(0.99)$ is used because that answer provides a 95.5-percent confidence interval. The earlier example of using an estimate of disposable personal income as \$600 million leading to a sales forecast of 9.44 million cars would be expanded to 9.44 $\pm$ 2(0.99) which is equal to a 95.5-percent confidence interval forecast of 7.46 to 11.42 million cars.

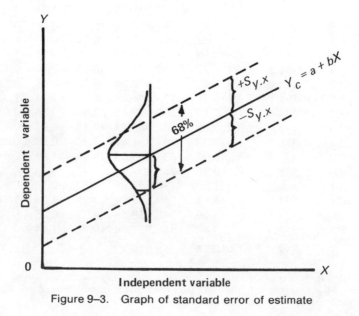

Figure 9–3.   Graph of standard error of estimate

MULTIPLE-REGRESSION ANALYSIS

More than one independent variable must typically be considered in the analysis of business change since the environment for business operations is a complex one. Certainly other variables in addition to disposable personal income are important in the influence of change in the new car sales example. Multiple-regression analysis is the measurement of a single dependent variable and a number of independent variables in combination to provide a basis for prediction. Continuing the example of new car sales, in addition to disposable income six variables are evaluated in the following multiple-regression computation to determine their significance to changes in new car sales. These variables are consumer credit, personal savings, number of new marriages, number of people employed, highway mileage, and number of family units. Data for these six additional variables are shown in Table 9–3.

Computation of Least Squares Equation

The solution of a multiple-regression equation is accomplished by the method of least squares in the same way as in the preceding solution of a simple-regression equation. The procedure is to solve for the unknowns in a group of simultaneous linear equations. Again there is one normal equation for each unknown in the problem. The results become the value for the constants in the multiple-regression equation.

Given the new car sales example with the independent variable of disposable personal income plus the six additional independent variables, the seven-variable linear multiple regression is

$$Y_c = a + b_1x_1 + b_2x_2 + b_3x_3 + b_4x_4 + b_5x_5 + b_6x_6 + b_7x_7$$

There are eight unknowns in the equation requiring simultaneous solution of eight normal equations. The computation of these normal equations would require a great deal of time and effort if performed manually. Another alternative is to utilize one of several prepared computer programs to solve for the linear multiple-regression equation by means of stepwise regression analysis. The reader is encouraged to review the solution of normal equations in the solution of simple-regression analysis so that he understands the concepts involved. The computer is programmed to examine each of the independent variables, one at a time, in relation to the dependent variable in a problem. The computer printout identifies the independent variables in the order of the extent of their relationship to the dependent variable. The computer solution also provides the value of each of the unknowns. The new car

TABLE 9-3

Empirical Data for Seven Variables Related to New Car Sales, 1950-1969

	New Car Sales (in millions) Y	Disposable Personal Income (in billions $) X	Number of Family Units (in millions)	Highway Mileage (in millions)	Personal Savings (in billions $)	Consumer Credit (in millions $)	Employment (in millions)	Marriages (in millions)
1951	5.3	227.5	39.9	3.3	17.7	22.7	60.8	1.6
	4.3	238.7	40.6	3.3	18.4	27.5	61.0	1.5
	6.1	252.5	40.8	3.4	20.0	31.4	61.9	1.5
	5.6	256.9	41.2	3.4	18.9	32.5	60.9	1.5
	8.0	274.4	41.9	3.4	17.5	38.9	62.9	1.5
1956	5.9	292.9	42.8	3.4	23.0	42.5	64.7	1.6
	6.4	308.8	43.4	3.5	23.1	45.3	65.0	1.5
	4.7	317.9	43.7	3.5	23.5	45.5	64.0	1.5
	6.3	337.3	44.2	3.5	23.6	52.1	65.6	1.5
	7.2	350.0	45.1	3.5	21.7	56.0	66.7	1.5
1961	5.8	364.7	45.4	3.6	27.3	57.7	66.8	1.5
	7.6	384.6	46.3	3.6	27.8	63.2	67.8	1.6
	8.0	402.5	47.0	3.6	27.5	69.9	68.8	1.7
	8.3	438.1	47.4	3.6	26.3	76.8	69.3	1.7
	9.7	473.2	47.8	3.7	28.4	90.3	71.1	1.8
1966	9.2	508.8	48.3	3.7	32.5	97.5	72.9	1.9
	8.1	546.3	48.9	3.7	40.4	102.1	74.4	1.9
	10.4	591.2	49.8	3.7	38.4	113.2	75.9	2.1
	10.2	631.6	50.5	3.7	37.6	122.5	77.9	2.1
	8.5	684.8	51.2	3.7	54.9	127.2	78.6	2.2

Source:: U.S. Department of Commerce. *Statistical Abstract of the United States,* Washington, D.C.: U.S. Government Printing Office, 1973.

sales data were run through a computer in a prepared program from the readily available *Statistical Package for the Social Sciences* (SPSS) Manual.[4] A complete computer printout is shown in Exhibit 9–1.

The linear multiple-regression equation for new car sales, as obtained from the computer printout, is

$$Y_c = -5.2848 + 0.1586X_1 - 0.1295X_2 + 3.4368X_3 - 0.0293X_4$$
$$+ 0.1173X_5 + 1.5489X_6 - 0.0446X_7$$

in which X_1 is consumer credit, X_2 is personal savings, X_3 is marriages, X_4 is disposable personal income, X_5 is employment, X_6 is highway mileage, and X_7 is number of family units. To forecast sales of new cars with the given equation, one would obtain data for the respective independent variables and solve for Y_c. If the year 1962 were selected, data taken from Table 9–3 would be substituted into the calculated equation, so

$$Y_c = -5.2848 + 0.1586(63.2) - 0.1295(27.8) + 3.4368(1.6)$$
$$- 0.0293(384.6) + 0.1173(67.8) + 1.5489(3.6) - 0.0446(46.3)$$

The solution 7.044 (millions of cars) estimated for year 1962 compared to the actual sales of 7.6 (millions of cars) in that year. The estimate should be modified to acknowledge the allowance for a standard error of estimate explained in the next section.

Standard Error of Estimate—Multiple Case

The standard error of estimate in the multiple case represents the closeness of the estimates to the empirical data just as in the case of the simple-regression analysis. It would be unusual for even multiple variables to provide a perfect basis for estimating the dependent variable. The standard error of estimate measures the deviation between the dependent variable and the computed values. Given that the values of the dependent variable are normally distributed about the regression plane, 68 percent of the values will tend to be in the range of the estimated value plus and minus one standard error of the estimate (see example below).

The calculation procedure for solving the standard error of estimate in the multiple case is the same as in the case of simple-regression analysis. It would be the square root of the summation of the empirical data minus the estimated data squared, all divided by the number of cases $[\sqrt{(Y - Y_c)/n}]$. These computations could be solved in the same manner as in the simple-regression example presented earlier. The

[4] Nie, N. H., Bent, D. H., and Hull, C. H. *Statistical Package for the Social Sciences.* New York: McGraw-Hill, 1970.

Exhibit 9–1. Multiple-regression analysis problem of new car sales

```
VOGELBACK COMPUTING CENTER
NORTHWESTERN UNIVERSITY

S P S S - - STATISTICAL PACKAGE FOR THE SOCIAL SCIENCES

VERSION 5.0 -- SPSS100 -- DECEMBER 15, 1972


RUN NAME           MULTIPLE REGRESSION ANALYSIS, 1951≠1970
VARIABLE LIST      SALES, DPI, FAMILY, MILEAGE, SAVINGS, CREDIT, JOBS, MARRIAGE
INPUT FORMAT       (8F4.1)
NO. OF CASES       20
VAR LABELS         SALES, NEW CAR SALES/
                   DPI, DISPOSABLE PERSONAL INCOME/
                   FAMILY, NUMBER OF FAMILY UNITS/
                   MILEAGE, HIGHWAY MILEAGE/
                   SAVINGS, PERSONAL SAVINGS/
                   CREDIT, CONSUMER CREDIT/
                   JOBS, EMPLOYMENT/
                   MARRIAGE, MARRIAGES/
REGRESSION         VARIABLES=SALES,DPI,FAMILY,MILEAGE,SAVINGS,CREDIT,JOBS,
                   MARRIAGE/ REGRESSION = SALES WITH DPI TO MARRIAGE(1)
STATISTICS         2
READ INPUT DATA
```

MINIMUM CM = 055100

132

```
*  *  *  *  *  *  *  *  *  *  *  *  *  *  *  *  *  *  *  *  *  *  *  *  *  *  *  *  *  *  *  *  *  *  *  *  *  *  *

DEPENDENT VARIABLE..   SALES      NEW CAR SALES

VARIABLE(S) ENTERED ON STEP NUMBER  1..   CREDIT      CONSUMER CREDIT


MULTIPLE R      .85331
R SQUARE        .72814
STD DEVIATION   .95518

------- VARIABLES IN THE EQUATION -------        --------- VARIABLES NOT IN THE EQUATION ---------
```

VARIABLE	B	BETA	STD ERROR B	F		VARIABLE	PARTIAL	TOLERANCE	F
CREDIT	.04648	.85331	.00669	48.21141		DPI	-.68412	.00693	14.95576
(CONSTANT)	4.19965					FAMILY	-.05008	.04363	.04274
						MILEAGE	-.11909	.14260	.24459
						SAVINGS	-.71246	.15369	17.52465
						JOBS	-.22495	.00866	.90609
						MARRIAGE	-.03365	.12701	.01928

```
*  *  *  *  *  *  *  *  *  *  *  *  *  *  *  *  *  *  *  *  *  *  *  *  *  *  *  *  *  *  *  *  *  *  *  *  *  *  *

VARIABLE(S) ENTERED ON STEP NUMBER  2..   SAVINGS      PERSONAL SAVINGS


MULTIPLE R      .93067
R SQUARE        .86614
STD DEVIATION   .68970

------- VARIABLES IN THE EQUATION -------        --------- VARIABLES NOT IN THE EQUATION ---------
```

VARIABLE	B	BETA	STD ERROR B	F		VARIABLE	PARTIAL	TOLERANCE	F
CREDIT	.09395	1.72502	.01233	58.08000		DPI	-.23510	.00214	.93606
SAVINGS	-.17925	-.94756	.04294	17.52465		FAMILY	-.20817	.04286	.72475
(CONSTANT)	6.00801					MILEAGE	-.09354	.13323	.14124
						JOBS	.01082	.00774	.00187
						MARRIAGE	.28510	.11450	1.41560

```
* * * * * * * * * * * * * * * * * * * * *        * * * * * * * * * * * * * * * * * * * *

DEPENDENT VARIABLE..    SALES    NEW CAR SALES

VARIABLE(S) ENTERED ON STEP NUMBER  3..    MARRIAGE    MARRIAGES


MULTIPLE R          .93649
R SQUARE           .87702
STD DEVIATION      .68142

---------- VARIABLES IN THE EQUATION ----------        ---------- VARIABLES NOT IN THE EQUATION ----------

VARIABLE        B          BETA      STD ERROR B      F              VARIABLE      PARTIAL    TOLERANCE       F

CREDIT       .08267      1.51790      .01544      28.68675          DPI          -.32463     .00202       1.76693
SAVINGS     -.19643     -1.03551      .04468      19.32862          FAMILY        .00707     .01901        .00075
MARRIAGE    2.34330      .30827      1.96950       1.41560          MILEAGE       .19456     .05706        .59016
(CONSTANT)  3.25872                                                 JOBS          .04954     .00761        .03690


* * * * * * * * * * * * * * * * * * * * * *        * * * * * * * * * * * * * * * * * * * *

VARIABLE(S) ENTERED ON STEP NUMBER  4..    DPI      DISPOSABLE PERSONAL INCOME


MULTIPLE R          .94339
R SQUARE           .88998
STD DEVIATION      .66565

---------- VARIABLES IN THE EQUATION ----------        ---------- VARIABLES NOT IN THE EQUATION ----------

VARIABLE        B          BETA      STD ERROR B      F              VARIABLE      PARTIAL    TOLERANCE       F

CREDIT       .19478      3.57612      .08567       5.16884          FAMILY        .02739     .01894        .01051
SAVINGS     -.11596     -.61131      .07463       2.41441          MILEAGE       .04731     .04400        .03140
MARRIAGE    2.96427      .38997      1.97984       2.24169          JOBS          .07501     .00758        .07922
DPI         -.03287     -2.53359      .02473       1.76693
(CONSTANT)  5.59119
```

134

* *

DEPENDENT VARIABLE.. SALES   NEW CAR SALES

VARIABLE(S) ENTERED ON STEP NUMBER 5.. JOBS   EMPLOYMENT

MULTIPLE R   .94371
R SQUARE   .89060
STD DEVIATION   .68707

--------- VARIABLES IN THE EQUATION --------- | --------- VARIABLES NOT IN THE EQUATION ---------

VARIABLE	B	BETA	STD ERROR B	F		VARIABLE	PARTIAL	TOLERANCE	F
CREDIT	.18165	3.33508	.09998	3.30114		FAMILY	.00328	.01696	.00014
SAVINGS	-.11951	-.63002	.07806	2.34423		MILEAGE	.05881	.04310	.04511
MARRIAGE	3.04503	.40059	2.06360	2.17737					
DPI	-.03334	-2.50993	.02558	1.69907					
JOBS	.09004	.26578	.31990	.07922					
(CONSTANT)	.49202								

* *

VARIABLE(S) ENTERED ON STEP NUMBER 6.. MILEAGE   HIGHWAY MILEAGE

MULTIPLE R   .94392
R SQUARE   .89098
STD DEVIATION   .71177

--------- VARIABLES IN THE EQUATION --------- | --------- VARIABLES NOT IN THE EQUATION ---------

VARIABLE	B	BETA	STD ERROR B	F		VARIABLE	PARTIAL	TOLERANCE	F
CREDIT	.16094	2.95497	.14223	1.28054		FAMILY	-.02990	.01278	.01074
SAVINGS	-.12723	-.67070	.08865	2.05973					
MARRIAGE	3.57666	.47053	3.29170	1.18063					
DPI	-.03030	-2.33583	.03011	1.01291					
JOBS	.10021	.31807	.33485	.08957					
MILEAGE	1.20036	.09369	5.65152	.04511					
(CONSTANT)	-4.96768								

135

```
* * * * * * * * * * * * * * * * * * * * * * * * * * * * * * * * * * * * * * * * * * *

DEPENDENT VARIABLE..    SALES    NEW CAR SALES

VARIABLE(S) ENTERED ON STEP NUMBER  7..    FAMILY    NUMBER OF FAMILY UNITS

MULTIPLE R          .94397
R SQUARE           .89107
STD DEVIATION      .74051

------------ VARIABLES IN THE EQUATION ------------          --------- VARIABLES NOT IN THE EQUATION ---------

VARIABLE        B          BETA       STD ERROR B      F        VARIABLE    PARTIAL    TOLERANCE      F

CREDIT        .15861      2.91217      .14967       1.12312
SAVINGS      -.12953      -.68285      .09487       1.86417
MARRIAGE     3.43680       .45213     3.68087        .87178
DPI          -.02929     -2.25802      .03281        .79744
JOBS          .11726       .37217      .38525        .09265
MILEAGE      1.54886       .12089     6.77334        .05229
FAMILY       -.04456      -.08735      .42994        .01074
(CONSTANT)   -5.28482

MAXIMUM STEP REACHED

* * * * * * * * * * * * * * * * * * * * * * * * * * * * * * * * * * * * * * * * * * *

DEPENDENT VARIABLE..    SALES    NEW CAR SALES

                                   SUMMARY TABLE

VARIABLE                          MULTIPLE R   R SQUARE   RSQ CHANGE   SIMPLE R       B          BETA

CREDIT      CONSUMER CREDIT          .85331      .72814     .72814      .85331       .15861      2.91217
SAVINGS     PERSONAL SAVINGS         .93067      .86614     .13799      .63937      -.12953      -.68285
MARRIAGE    MARRIAGES                .93649      .87702     .01088      .79103      3.43680       .45213
DPI         DISPOSABLE PERSONAL INCOME  .94339   .88998     .01296      .82065      -.02929     -2.25802
JOBS        EMPLOYMENT               .94371      .89060     .00062      .83870       .11726       .37217
MILEAGE     HIGHWAY MILEAGE          .94392      .89098     .00038      .81358      1.54886       .12089
FAMILY      NUMBER OF FAMILY UNITS   .94397      .89107     .00010      .82904      -.04456      -.08735
(CONSTANT)                                                                          -5.28482
```

136

typical computer printout obviates the need for this calculation because it performs the task in the prepared program and presents the answer in the printout. Exhibit 9–1 shows the standard error of estimate of the multiple-regression equation for new car sales to be 0.7118. Therefore the range for including about 68 percent of the actual number of new cars sold is $Y_c \pm 0.712$. Referring back to the example of estimating sales of new cars for 1962, the 68-percent range would be 7.044 ± 0.712 or $6.332 - 7.756$. This range would encompass the actual sales figure of 7.6 (millions of cars) in 1962.

Partial-Regression Coefficient

Each coefficient in the multiple-regression equation is called a "partial-regression" coefficient and it shows the average change in the dependent variable relative to a unit change in each respective independent variable. In the multiple-regression equation for new cars, the value $0.1586X_1$ is interpreted to mean that there is a change of 0.1586 car sales (in millions of units) for every unit change X_1, which is consumer credit in billions of dollars. Likewise, the second most important variable and coefficient, $-0.1295X_2$ is interpreted to mean that there is a reverse effect of personal savings on new car sales. There is a change of -0.1295 car sales (in millions of units) for every unit change in personal savings (in billions of dollars). A manager can analyze the different coefficients for their relationship to the variable.

Beta Coefficient

Since the b values in the multiple-regression equation are usually expressed in different units, such as population versus dollars, it is necessary to standardize these values to comparable pure numbers. One way to do this is to adjust each value to a beta coefficient, that is, to express each value in units of its own standard deviation. The method is

$$\beta_1 = b_1 \sqrt{\frac{S_{x1}}{S_y}}$$

The importance of each b value and its respective independent variable varies directly with the size of its beta coefficient: The larger the beta-coefficient value, the more important the relationship of the independent variable. In the preceding illustration the beta coefficients in Exhibit 9–1 are 2.91 for consumer credit, 0.68 for personal savings, 0.45 for marriages, 2.25 for disposable personal income, 0.37 for jobs, 0.12 for mileage, and 0.09 for family. By comparison, consumer credit and disposable personal income have the highest beta coefficients. They are the most important of the seven problem variables in the determination of new car sales.

Application of Regression Analysis

Use in forecasting. A regression equation, which shows the relationship between two or more variables, provides the basis for prediction. Given a certain relationship, one can ask what would be the value of a dependent variable if the value of related independent variables are known? The illustrative example in this chapter has been a forecast of new car sales. Other developments of forecasting by regression analysis are found in companies like Eli Lilly, Monsanto, and RCA.[5] Another type of application involves determination of factors that are related to profits. In a recent study of ski-area profitability an effort was made to pinpoint factors that explain the existing wide range of financial success experienced by 34 ski areas in the Rocky Mountain area.[6] Alternative factors to be analyzed in the study were derived from an analysis of (1) skier wants, since a ski area must attract customers in order to make a profit; (2) business economics, since ski areas are in economic competition with each other and also with other forms of recreation; and (3) views of owners and operators, since they have developed insight into the significant variables leading to profitable operations. Regression analysis in the study indicated that the most significant factors were (1) age of ski area, (2) the number of days the area was open during a season, and (3) the average lift capacity utilizations. Specifically, each extra year of ski-area age and each four-to-six additional days of operation were related to adding one extra percentage point increase in rate of return on ski-area revenue. In addition the study results showed that increasing capacity utilization by 4 percent also is related to about one percentage point increase in rate of revenue return. The factors that lacked significance in explaining profitability in the ski-area study were variables for price, size, lift quality (ratio of number of chair lifts and gondolas to the total number of tows and lifts), snow depth, daily temperature, slope difficulty, vertical drop, and nearness to population. The author of the study is quick to point out inherent limitations in his methodology, but for the data available, the regression analysis serves to indicate significant variables in explaining change of profitability among ski-area operations.

CORRELATION ANALYSIS

The coefficient of correlation r is a statistical measure used to determine the closeness of the relationship between variables. Value of

---

[5] Levy, Robert. A clearer crystal ball. *Dun's Review*, 98(July, 1971): 51.

[6] Bechter, Dan M. Ski area profitability. *Federal Reserve Bank of Kansas City Monthly Review*, March, 1972.

the coefficient of correlation ranges between $+1$ and -1. Correlation is positive when the change in value of a dependent variable is directly related to a change in value of an independent variable. The reverse situation would be true in negative correlation; the change in value of a dependent variable is related to an opposite change in the value of an independent variable. The extreme value of "one" occurs if there is perfect correlation between two variables. Of course if there is zero regression, there will be zero correlation and $r = 0$. The square of the coefficient of correlation r^2 is known as the "coefficient of determination," which measures the change in a dependent variable as explained by an independent variable in regression analysis. These concepts will be explained below.

Computation of Coefficient of Correlation

Plotting of the relationship of variables on a scatter diagram containing lines corresponding to $\overline{X}$ and $\overline{Y}$, as in Figure 9–4, is useful to correlation analysis. Visual examination indicates the position of points in different quadrants.[7] In positive regression, most of the points would be located in quadrants I and III, whereas the points would be located primarily in quadrants II and IV if the case were one of negative regression. A sum of the products of the variation $(X - \overline{X})$ called x and the variation $(Y - \overline{Y})$ called y is an indicator of the correlation of correlation. However, it is necessary to divide Σxy by the standard deviations of S_x and S_y in order to standardize the values of s and y so that the bias of units involved is eliminated. For example, a value of x and y expressed in tons would yield a result that is 2000 times larger than the same situation expressed in terms of pounds, yet the closeness of the relationship is the same. Therefore the equation for solving the coefficient of correlation is

$$r = \frac{\Sigma xy}{n \cdot S_x \cdot S_y}$$

Since

$$S_x = \sqrt{\frac{\Sigma x^2}{n}} \quad \text{and} \quad S_y = \sqrt{\frac{\Sigma y^2}{n}}$$

then by substitution

$$r = \frac{\Sigma xy}{\sqrt{\Sigma x^2} \cdot \sqrt{\Sigma y^2}}$$

---

[7] Chance, William. *Statistical Methods for Decision Making*. Homewood, Ill.: R. D. Irwin, 1969 (p. 266).

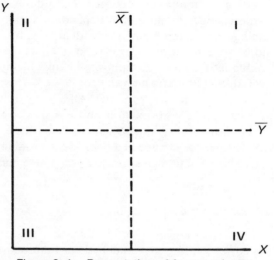

Figure 9–4.   Presentation of four quadrants

terms for which values may easily be computed in regression analysis. Referring to data in the new car sales illustration in Table 9–3,

$$r = \frac{\Sigma xy}{\sqrt{\Sigma x^2} \cdot \sqrt{\Sigma y^2}}$$

$$= \frac{3826.26}{\sqrt{359,142.23} \cdot \sqrt{60.41}}$$

$$= \frac{3826.26}{(599.28)(7.77)}$$

$$= \frac{3826.26}{4656.41}$$

$$= 0.82$$

An r value of 0.82 indicates a high relationship between new car sales and disposable personal income.

Computation of the Coefficient of Determination

After a regression line has been determined, it is possible to compute the degree of variation explained by the independent variable s in the regression analysis by computing a coefficient of determination. The basic factors involved are shown in Figure 9–5. The computed regression value Y_c is based on the relationship of Y on X, so the deviation of Y_c from Y is explained by X. However, the residual of actual value Y from Y_c is not explained by X but is due to other reasons. If the residual is large, then other independent variables should be examined to determine additional relationships.

The computation of the coefficient of determination is

$$r^2 = \frac{\text{explained variation}}{\text{total variation}} = \frac{\Sigma(Y_c - \overline{Y})^2}{\Sigma(Y - \overline{Y})^2}$$

Through mathematical substitution the equation becomes

$$r^2 = \frac{(\Sigma xy)^2}{\Sigma x^2 \, \Sigma y^2}$$

which turns out to be the square of the coefficient of correlation. In the new car sales illustration

$$r^2 = (0.82)^2 = 0.6724$$

indicating that slightly over 67 percent of the variation in new car sales is explained by variation in personal disposable income. Changes in other variables would have to be examined to explain the residual variation of about 33 percent (100 to 67.24 percent).

Coefficient of Multiple Determination and Multiple Correlation

In most business problem situations, analysis of more than one independent variable is required in order to explain a sufficiently large percentage of the change in a dependent variable. As seen in the

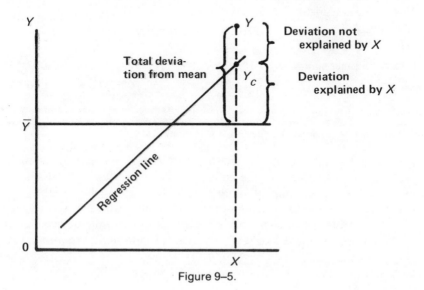

Figure 9–5.

TABLE 9–4

Relationship Between New Car Sales and Disposable Personal Income

	New Car Sales (in millions of units)	Disposable Personal Income (in billions of dollars)	XY	X²	Y²
1951	5.3	227.5	1,205.75	51,756.25	28.09
1952	4.3	238.7	1,026.41	56,977.69	18.49
1953	6.1	252.5	1,540.25	63,756.25	37.21
1954	5.6	256.9	1,438.64	65,997.61	31.36
1955	8.0	274.4	2,195.20	75,295.36	64.00
1956	5.9	292.9	1,728.11	85,790.41	34.81
1957	6.4	308.8	1,976.32	95,357.44	40.96
1958	4.7	317.9	1,494.13	101,060.41	22.09
1959	6.3	337.3	2,124.99	113,771.29	39.69
1960	7.2	350.0	2,520.00	122,500.00	51.84
1961	5.8	364.7	2,115.26	133,006.09	33.64
1962	7.3	384.6	2,807.58	147,917.16	53.29
1963	8.0	402.5	3,220.00	162,066.25	64.00
1964	8.3	438.1	3,636.23	191,931.61	68.89
1965	9.7	473.2	4,590.04	223,918.24	94.09
1966	9.2	508.8	4,680.96	258,877.44	84.64
1967	8.1	546.3	4,425.03	298,443.69	65.61
1968	10.4	591.2	6,148.48	349,517.44	108.16
1969	10.0	631.6	6,316.00	398,918.56	100.00
1970	8.5	684.8	5,820.80	468,951.04	72.25
Sum	145.1	7,882.7	61,010.18	3,465,714.23	1,113.11
Mean	7.255	394.135			
Less mean times sum			57,183.91	3,106,572.00	1,052.70
Adjusted sum		(Σxy)	$3,826.27(\Sigma x^2)$	$359,142.23(\Sigma y^2)$	60.41

Source: U.S. Department of Commerce. *Statistical Abstract of the United States.* Washington, D.C.: U.S. Government Printing Office, 1972; and *Automobile Facts and Figures.* Detroit, Mich.: Automobile Manufacturing Association, 1972.

preceding section, change in the disposable personal income variable explained 67.24 percent of the change in new car sales. It is possible to examine the relationship of more than one independent variable to a dependent variable and thereby increase the percentage of change that can be explained. The result is the coefficient of multiple determination R^2, which is computed like the coefficient of determination above,

$$R^2 = \frac{\text{explained variation}}{\text{unexplained variation}}$$

For example, in the new car sales illustration, when six additional independent variables were analyzed along with disposable personal income in Exhibit 9–1, R^2 was raised to 0.891. Actually the three most significant factors of consumer credit, personal savings, and number of new marriages changed the above R^2 value of 0.67 to 0.877.

The coefficient of multiple correlation R indicates the closeness of the relationship between the dependent variable and two or more independent variables. In the new car sales illustration, analysis of the three variables of consumer credit, personal income, and number of new marriages changed the coefficient of correlation r from 0.82 to the coefficient of multiple correlation R of 0.936. This value obviously indicates a high degree of closeness between the sale of new cars and the independent variables.

Application to Sales Management Analysis

Regression and correlation analyses are also effective for evaluating sales territory performance. The typical sales manager is interested in evaluating performance of his salesmen and in predicting sales performance. It has been possible for managers to establish quotas and to predict sales on the basis of indicators selected by executive judgment. Regression and correlation analyses, on the other hand, form a much more sophisticated approach, which is able to identify variables that influence territory sales and to indicate the relative importance of each variable.

A specific example shows how sales for one large manufacturer in 25 territories are analyzed.[8] Independent variables were selected as determinants of sales territory performance: market potential measured by industry sales in territory, P; average workload per account, W; total number of accounts assigned to a salesman, A; salesman experience, S_e; salesman motivation and effort, S_p; market share, M_s; market share change over previous four years, M_c; and advertising expenditures in territory, A_d. Stepwise multiple-regression analysis on a computer produced the following equation:

$$\text{territory sales} = -1051 + 12.13A + 0.02P + 447.15M_c + 61.53W$$
$$+ 157.09S_p - 6.2M_s + 1.08S_e + 0.004A_d$$

Thus the manufacturer has a mathematical equation by which he can predict future sales in each territory. A comparison of actual sales in each territory to predicted sales provides the basis for an evaluation of sales efficiency in territories. Salesmen in territories that exceed pre-

---

[8] Example is based upon the article by Cravens, D. W., Woodruff, R. B., and Stamper, J. C. An analytical approach for evaluating sales territory performance. *Journal of Marketing*, 36(January, 1972): 31–37.

dicted sales may be rewarded and analyzed for successful practices. Conversely, weak sales territories will become evident and can be isolated for special management attention.

The importance of the independent variables is shown in Table 9–5. The multiple correlation coefficient between territory sales and the independent variables is shown as 0.85 and the coefficient of determination is 0.72. From a practical standpoint, the first three independent variables were the primary factors in the explained variation of territory sales.

Caution should be taken in applying regression and correlation analyses to territory sales analysis. Analysis may not be appropriate for a firm that has territories with different individualized determinants of sales. In addition, analysis does not lend itself to a firm that is undergoing very rapid short-run growth. Cravens lists three requirements for appropriate measures of the independent variables: "(1) The measure should adequately describe the variable as it exists in each territory (validity); (2) the measure should provide an adequate description over an acceptable period of time (reliability); and (3) the measure should make data demands that can be satisfied by the firm's data source."[9]

TABLE 9–5

Summary of Stepwise Multiple-Regression Analysis

Step Number	Variable Entered	R	R^2	Increase in R^2
1	Number of accounts	0.75	0.57	0.57
2	Industrial sales	0.80	0.64	0.07
3	Market share change	0.83	0.69	0.05
4	Workload per account	0.84	0.71	0.02
5	Performance of salesman	0.85	0.72	0.01
6	Market share	0.85	0.72	Insignificant
7	Salesman experience	0.85	0.72	Insignificant
8	Advertising expenditures	0.85	0.72	Insignificant

---

[9] *Ibid.*, p. 37.

CHAPTER 10

Future Computer Developments for Decision Making

Future developments in the computer industry promise to bring increased assistance to executive decision-making procedure. The increased assistance will be in terms of greater speed, greater efficiency, and lower cost. Criteria for measuring the anticipated change are hardware installations and operations, development in software, and evolution of problem applications.

DEVELOPMENT OF HARDWARE INSTALLATIONS AND OPERATIONS

The number of computers sold is indicative of the growth pattern of the industry. There were approximately 1000 computers delivered in 1961; about 20,000 units delivered in 1971; and expectations of about 50,000 computers to be delivered in 1980.[1] The power capacity has had an even greater growth experience. The total computer power in the United States was about a half-million additions per second in 1955 and 200 million per second in 1965. The expected growth through 1975 is an increase of about 400-fold over 1965.[2]

The make-up of the computer installations has been changing and should continue to do so. There has been an increasing number of remote terminal devices for each computer installed. It is predicted that these devices will represent about 50 percent of the total peripheral equipment market, with about 3 million terminals in use by 1980.[3]

---

[1] Thierauf, R. J. *Data Processing for Business and Management*. New York: Wiley, 1973 (p. 640).

[2] Developments in computer technology. *Computing Newsletter*, ed. J. Daniel Couger, University of Colorado. (November, 1972): 3.

[3] Thierauf, *op. cit.*, p. 640.

This computer resource should have a significant effect on improving management decision making.

The cost of operating a computer has been decreasing steadily. It cost about $1000 to do a million operations on a keyboard in 1945; less than 6 cents to run that job in 1972; and the cost in 1975 is expected to be a fraction of a cent (0.6 of a cent). Storage cost has had a parallel decline: In the period 1955–1965 the storage cost to perform 1 million operations was $10, and it is predicted that storage cost will decline to about 5 cents for the same number of operations in 1975.[4] A diagram of these computer developments is shown in Figure 10–1.

There are a series of technical improvements being predicted for computer operations, which should stimulate usage. One of the most promising is the use of the laser, which has the ability to store data compactly. A description of laser-based computers is as follows:

> The laser has the capability of storing about one million bits per square inch of film. Laser-based computers, featuring many trillion bits of memory, will be common. Its basic principle storage is the 0-bit and 1-bit combination of any binary system. It records a 1-bit by concentrating a very small beam of light for an extremely short period of time, which results in "burning the emulsion." The laser reads data by sensing the white and black spots (0 or 1).[5]

An executive overview of computer evolution is shown in Figure 10–2. The laser-based computer would be classified in the future generations category.

Another very promising technical development in the future is that of tiny magnetic "bubbles" or "domains."[6] These magnetic bubbles are the potential basis for improved compactness and inexpensive data storage and processing. The new technology consists of thin slices of magnetizable crystals grown from mixtures of iron or lead oxides and rare-earth metals, which can store as many as a million bits of information per square inch. It is estimated that the new technology might store millions of words and numbers in a volume the size of a few cigarette packages. The present technology would require units the size of clothes closets to store the same equivalent information. The devices have other advantages such as no moving parts to wear out, little heat generated, very low power needed for operations, and little wiring

---

[4] Developments in computer technology, *op. cit.*, p. 3.

[5] Thierauf, *op. cit.*, p. 642.

[6] Descriptive data was obtained from Thierauf, *op. cit.*, p. 642.

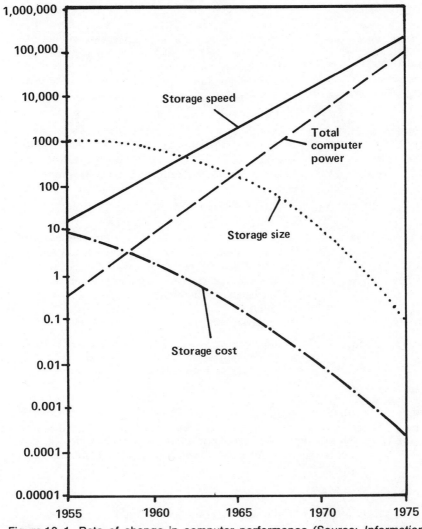

Figure 10–1. Rate of change in computer performance (Source: *Information Technology: Some Critical Implications for Decision Makers.* The Conference Board, Inc., 1972, p. 188.)

Computer Generation	Some Distinguishing New Technical Features	Systems Approach
Future generations	Significant simplification of systems analysis and programming Increased reliability Confidentialness	Extension of vital decision-making process Data banks of internal and external information
Third generation	Compatibility Micromonolothic circuitry Mass storage Real-time and time-sharing Operating systems Multiprogramming and processing	Large-scale systems Logistics applications Company-wide systems Total systems approaches
Second generation	Transistors Magnetic tape Expanded magnetic core Some use of higher symbolic languages including COBOL Data transmission	Segments of new management information system Management science applications
First generation	Vacuum tubes Limited magnetic core Machine and assembly language coding Electronic Stored program	Conversion of existing applications

Figure 10–2. An executive overview of computer evolution (Source: Tomeski, Edward A. *The Computer Revolution*. London: Macmillan, 1970 [p. 132])

needed to interconnect them. The net outcome would be a vast reduction in the cost of storing and handling data.

DEVELOPMENTS IN SOFTWARE

Software designers have improved available software at a steady rate, but they tend to lag behind computer hardware developments. The extent of the problem is indicated by the development of software for a particular generation of computers being realized only after a new generation has been announced. There are predictions of improvement in the lag problem with potential future developments in software. These improvements include human language programming, development of firmware, and computer ability to "solve" problems.

Human Language Programming

Probably the most promising research in improving the effectiveness of computer software is the research being done on direct human conversation with the computer. The goal is to enable users to interact with a computer through voice instructions instead of the complicated written languages that are used currently. Researchers at Bell Telephone Laboratories have completed a system that converts text input into synthetic speech:

> Words input through a teletype are automatically produced as "nearly natural sounding" synthetic speech. The experimental work takes advantage of an improved understanding of speech patterns. The computer is provided with mathematical approximations for the shapes and motions the human vocal tract assumes when uttering common sounds and sound sequences. It is also provided with a basic dictionary of word categories and definitions in digital form. Rules of timing, pitch, and stress which people use naturally in everyday conversation are also approximated.
>
> When words are inputed, the system analyzes the sentence, assigns stress and timing to each word, and finds a phonetic description of each word in the dictionary. Mathematical descriptions of vocal tract motions are then computed, converted to a signal, and generated as electrical speech signals which may be heard over a loudspeaker or telephone. Users of this new technique include a doctor desiring the recitation of a page from a medical book, a stock manager seeking information about inventory or an airline clerk looking for flight information.[7]

The ability of researchers to achieve human language programming would reduce the lag that exists between hardware and software developments.

---

[7] *Ibid.*, p. 644.

Development of Firmware

One effort to speed up the programming process is the increased development of firmware, which is a form of a microprogram. Many of the functions that are now performed by software can be included in the firmware of the computer, relieving the programmer of writing instruction for those functions. The computer would have stored logic to enable it to execute elementary operations without specific written instructions. The results of an expansion of firmware would directly accelerate the development of software.

Computer Ability to "Solve" Problems

Interesting research is being conducted to develop computer capability to actually learn how to solve problems instead of merely following instructions. The desired development is to enable the computer to self-learn and thereby self-program in the problem-solving process. There is speculation that by the year 2000, computers are likely to match or simulate some of man's creative capacities.[8] At the present time computers are engaging in competitive activities with man, for example, playing chess games.

EVOLUTION OF PROBLEM APPLICATIONS

Application of the computer in the future will tend toward the challenge of undertaking problems that are more comprehensive in scope. Computer utilization in the business world is evolving toward what is called "data-managed" systems; computer service centers are evolving into computer utilities; an electronic money system is possible; and the organizational structure of firms is changing.

Data-Managed Systems

The design of future management information systems is likely to emphasize a broader perspective of the organization structure concerned with the management of the entire corporation at the corporate level. This new approach is an outgrowth of the current applications in the functional areas of a business or the management of business operations at the divisional level. The primary benefit of a more comprehensive approach to decision making is the synergistic efficiency. Top man-

---

[8] Kahn, Herman, and Wiener, Anthony J. *The Year 2000: A Framework for Speculation.* New York: Macmillan, 1967 (p. 89).

agement will be in a position to analyze ramifications of decisions throughout the business enterprise, rather than only in one, or a few, departments.

The expectation is that progress toward developed data-managed systems will be slow. Need is for mathematical models that deal with overall optimization of the firm. Current computers cannot possibly handle the storage needs for a mathematical model of entire firms. The increased storage capacity in future generations of computers would probably supply the needs of more comprehensive problems.

Computer Utilities

The computer utility is a single firm that offers many services to computer users, which are presently being supplied by a number of firms. The single firm would integrate computer activities now undertaken on a separate basis. Included in the service would be systems development work, programming, time sharing, optical scanning, real-time processing, remote batch processing, financing, leasing, and the manufacturing of peripheral hardware.[9]

Electronic Money System

The developments in hardware, software, and systems will make the feasibility of an electronic money system possible. The system would work as follows:

An electronic money system would have all forms and institutions linked together in a massive data processive system. The entire system would be linked by a vast communication network [Figure 10–3]. A data processing banking center would be used to clear claims (equivalent to invoices) against accepted claims (equivalent to payments). Basically, the system would operate as follows. The vendor submits invoices to one of the regional clearing centers. Similarly, the customer submits a list of claims that he is willing to pay. Both the claims and the accepted claims can be transmitted to the data processing banking center in machine language. Payment could be made by means of a clearing operation. The net effect would be an elimination of checks.

An essential part of electronic money would be a firm's payroll. Instead of the individual receiving his payroll check

---

[9] Thierauf, *op. cit.*, p. 645.

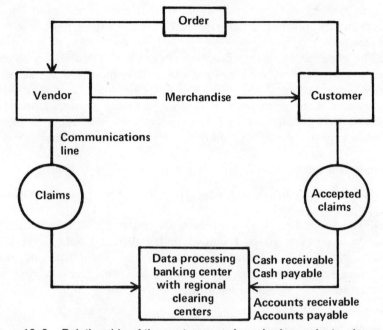

Figure 10–3.   Relationship of the customer and vendor in an electronic money
               system (Source: Thierauf, R. J. *Data Processing for Business
               and Management.* New York: Wiley, 1972 [p. 646])

periodically, his salary less all legitimate deductions would be
written electronically on tape. This tape from the company's
office would be fed to a computer at the payee's bank and
entered as a deposit. The computer at the individual's bank
would automatically pay all his recurring bills (generally on a
monthly basis) which include payments on a home, a car,
insurance policies, department store accounts, and similar
items. Likewise, the computer will transfer the excess bank
balance to a savings account, mutual fund, stock account, or
some other authorized account.

    Under an electronic money system, the individual would
be able to handle daily transactions without physically utilizing paper money. This can be accomplished by having
everyone carry a small plastic card that contains a voice
pattern on the card itself. (Since everyone has a voice
pattern–about unique as one's fingerprints, the bank's computer will test for the correct voice pattern before accepting

a charge for goods or services.) The seller will insert the plastic card in a reading device that will identify the individual and voice at the customer's bank via the computer. If sufficient cash is available in the customer's account, the seller will ring up the sale which transfers the appropriate amount from the customer's account to the seller's account. If the customer has insufficient funds, the bank's computer can arrange a loan on the spot. On the other hand, if the customer prefers to let the bill run for a period of time, say to the end of the month (allowable by the seller), the transaction will be so recorded at the customer's bank. The seller will record the sale, but will not have funds switched until the date agreed upon.

To determine the balance of one's account, the individual would slip his plastic card into a videophone terminal (installed in his home) and key in the appropriate code numbers. After a quick identity check of number and voice pattern, the computer is ready for the request. The person would enter a request to view his up-to-the-minute bank balance which would be flashed on the viewing screen. The visual display unit would generally include: bank balance, saving account amount, mutual fund holdings, stock holdings, home mortgage balance, payments made in the last week, pre-arranged payments due the next week, and projection of deposits from employer for payroll check. This current visual information would assist the individual in deciding whether or not additional large purchases could be made without jeopardizing his financial position.

Before this electronic money system can operate, there must be full acceptance of such a card by all banks of the country which must be linked into one credit card system. This is necessary since a store that keeps its account at one bank must accept the card of a person who keeps his account at another. The use of an "Interbank Card" whereby all banks in the United States would honor each other's cards is required. However, this problem is not as complex as obtaining public acceptance of this national system. For one thing, banks have been selling people on the idea of getting a receipt for everything they buy through canceled checks. Now this concept must be undone. All in all, the psychological barriers are much greater than the technical problems. Perhaps in about 20 years all facets of the checkless society will have been assembled and operating in an efficient manner for most individuals in the United States.[10]

Changing Organization Structure

The trend toward development of larger computer systems within companies will likely result in fewer decision-making executives and a growing number of specialists. The expectation is for increased use of a project approach whereby a group of people with various skills are brought together to work on a specific assignment and then regroup on completion of the project. When the project has been completed, there is a need for the traditional hierarchy of organization to implement the results. The outcome appears to be a blending of the project approach and of the usual line and staff structure.

Forecasts dealing with job content of managers are the following:[11]

1. Managerial jobs will continue to develop a higher and higher research content.
2. There will be a continued upgrading in skills.
3. The need for managers to develop computer-related skills will increase.

The logical development will be for managers to concentrate on doing the things that they can do better than the computers and vice versa. Managers can emphasize creative tasks and determine goal setting, which involves values and preferences. The computer should be given the responsibility of doing the computational work. Both should be active in the communications function: the manager stressing the human motivation aspects of communications and the computer conducting the task associated aspects of communications. Anticipated developments in the computer industry should enable the manager to improve his decision-making ability significantly.

---

[10] *Ibid.*, pp. 646, 647.
[11] Whisler, Thomas L. *The Impact of Computers on Organizations.* New York: Praeger, 1970 (p. 148).

Index

155